The Ivy League Writi

Guaranteed

to Help You Write the Perfect College Research Paper

A Step-by-Step Guide for Science, Technology, Engineering, Pharmacy, Medicine and Math Majors

Volume I

The Ivy League Writing Guide: Guaranteed to Help You Write the Perfect College Research Paper. A Step-by-Step Guide for Science, Technology, Engineering, Pharmacy, Medicine and Math Majors

Copyright © August 2017 by Cheryl R. Carter

All rights reserved.
No part of this book may be reproduced in any form or by any electronic or mechanical means, including information storage and retrieval systems, without permission in writing from the author. The only exception is by a reviewer, who may quote short excerpts in a review.

Printed in the United States of America

ISBN-13:978 1975963323

ISBN 10: 1975963326

The Ivy League Writing Guide:
Guaranteed
to Help You Write the Perfect College Research Paper

A Step-by-Step Guide for Science, Technology, Engineering, Pharmacy, Medicine and Math Majors

Cheryl R. Carter

Long Island, New York

USA

About this Guide:

This guide is specifically directed to international college learners. Students currently enrolled in college will also find this guide particularly valuable, while those in high school will discover this writing method provides them with a ubiquitous advantage over other college freshmen.

In fact, most students, especially those majoring in science, engineering, math medicine, technology or pharmacy, will find this writing method makes composing papers easy.

This composition process is taught systematically: and thus makes the college paper writing process easy to understand and enables students to get better grades. This writing method produces clear and well-organized essays, research papers and compositions.

STEM learners will particularly appreciate the easy follow-the-format composition method of this guide, since it appeals to scientific, technical and mathematical thinking.

The approach is quite comprehensive, and yet at the same time simplistic enough to help all struggling writers not just those majoring in the sciences. International student writers and STEM writers have thrived using this writing approach. Nearly, all writers will find this approach viable.

Volume I specifically addresses the research paper which is applicable to nearly any college class that a STEM student would take in college.

Volume 2 addresses English and liberal arts papers. Specifically, these volumes help the student write powerful and purposeful papers that do not appear or sound like they are following a formula. Graduate students have also found these volumes helpful when completing their writing assignments.

"Teachers open the door. You enter by yourself. .... 师傅领进门，修行在个人 [師傅領進門，修行在個人] Shī fu lǐng jìn mén, xiū xíng zài gè rén."

Dedication:

For Gregory, Joy, Talitha, Mason and Mekhai

Writing is simply thinking on paper.

Table of Contents

Part One: Laying the Foundation

Goals 2
How to Implement *this Guide* 5

Part Two: The Writing Process

The Writing Process.. 8
Thesis Statements 12
Structuring Paragraphs.. 21
Taking Notes for Stronger Arguments 31
Citations in your Writing 43
Argumentative Writing.. 53
Final Instructions for College Assignments 56
College Reading Strategies 68

Part Three Research Writing

Research Paper Basics 75
Topical Paper.. 77
Research Précis 79
High School Research Paper.. 81
College Research Paper... 85

Part Four: Graphic Organizers

Sample Graphic Organizers.. 95

Sample Essays 98

Part Five

A Complete Grammar and Style Review Guide 112

Part One
Laying the Foundation

"Learning is a treasure that will follow its owner everywhere… 学习是永远跟随主人的宝物 [學習是永遠跟隨主人的寶物] Xuéxí shì yǒngyuǎn gēnsuí zhǔrén de bǎowù]"

Goals

- To instill a love for writing such that learners become better writers.
- To utilize writing in all subjects and disciplines so the writing process becomes natural and easy for learners.
- To have learners exceed established national writing standards.
- To prepare learners for college writing assignments.
- To develop higher-level thinking skills in all curriculum areas.
- To strengthen grammar, punctuation, and sentence structure using a learner's own writing as a foundation.
- To make writing instruction easier for all learners.

Cheryl R. Carter

Introduction

Overwhelmingly, time and time again, research has shown the ability to write well is key to overall college success. This is no surprise. After all, writing at its core is thinking on paper, and the ability to think and reason is what separates great learners from mediocre performers. In my transition from high school teacher to college professor, I have noted five distinct differences in high school and college writing. If each of these differences were addressed, students, especially adult students-- those returning to school after a long absence, would make a smoother transition to college level work because writing is needed for almost every class.

One

High school students write papers that are informative whereas college papers are explorative.

College students are expected to be embrace new concepts and expand upon those ideas in their papers. Most high school papers are generally informative. A high school teacher generally assigns learners papers to check for their understanding. For instance, a high school teacher might ask a student to write a paper on the Civil War. The student is expected to regurgitate facts and ideologies discussed in class. A history professor, on the other hand, wants the student to discover new ideologies about the Civil War that were not discussed or explored in class. Furthermore, the student may be asked to research another war and note political, economic or other similarities to the Civil War.

Two

High school students write general thesis statements, whereas college students are expected to form solid argumentative thesis statements.

In high school students wrote very general thesis statements, if they wrote them at all. Students might write: I am going to discuss the way Romeo and Juliet interacted with their families. However, a college thesis is much more specific and directive and really drives the paper. For instance, a college thesis might be: It will be proven that the friar's lack of religious influence caused the death of Romeo. The college thesis should be opinionated and it should be written in such a way that it could be challenged by someone with an opposing view.

Three

High school students may surf the web and find sources to use in their paper whereas college professors will only accept scholarly research sources.

In high school students googled and used popular sources like magazines, websites and books in their papers. For the most part, if learners did not plagiarize, these sources were accepted as authoritative. College writing, on the other hand, requires the use of scholarly sources. Scholarly sources are research references that are peer-reviewed or an articles or books from an academic publisher. A website has to meet certain criteria to be scholarly.

Four

High school students were taught to write in a simple form, whereas college writing requires more invention.

In high school most students were taught to write the typical five paragraph essay. This essay generally included an introduction, conclusion and three body paragraphs and each body paragraph elaborated on each point. This was the way most learners prepared for the writing portion of the SAT. In College writing students are expected to write expansively and decipher each point, and the five paragraph essay just does not meet the standard.

Five

High school students write papers using a loose form of MLA or generally no form at all, whereas college professors require strict adherence to form.

Students should know how to cite in Modern Language Association (MLA), Association of

Psychological (APA), Chicago, etc. The font should always be 12 point. The research within the paper should be cited a specific way.

These five areas, if addressed will help learners to write well in college and beyond. Adult learners, especially those returning to school and those taking online classes, often struggle repeatedly with some of these issues. However, once learners master these skills they quickly transform into strong learners

This guide addresses all these areas. The process is systematic. Many learners struggle with writing essays and therefore need a framework on which to build. These learners like the step-by-step approach in this book. Both reluctant and intuitive writers like the writing process *because a* structure relieves many learners of the pressure of how to start an assignment. In particular struggling writers like this guide because it takes the guess work out of writing assignments.

The method has also relieved many parents who want to ensure their children are ready for the rigors of college learning. Research has shown writing and critical reading the two key skills necessary for college success, no matter what your child chooses to study in college.

Implementing This Approach

Writing is a form of communication. It is simply the ability to turn an idea into words that convey a clear message. In its most basic form, writing is simply an idea that morphs into a message. An effective message is one that resonates with the reader.

Writing is merely the compilation of ideas organized in such a way that the reader is inspired, Structured writing can guide a learner in his thinking process because he is forced to organize his thoughts within the writing form framework. This combination of approaches is what makes this writing instruction so effective.

These learners will also be able to complete their writing assignments more quickly because the steps are uncomplicated and straightforward. Learners will know what to do because the format is very simple. Many learners want to know how to approach a writing assignment. They need a format. Form is an essential skill in academic writing

The basic elements of this curriculum are important to a learner's writing success. A successful writing learner is not intimidated by writing assignments, but instead actively engages with new ideas and is uninhibited when it comes to sharing writing with others in the college classroom, on an editorial page, or in a published work. These methods also build a learner's confidence.

Cheryl R. Carter

How to Approach this Guide

Where do I begin?

You should understand the basics of the approach and grading criteria. Journaling assignments should be graded for content only. However, format writing should be graded for the form, content, and adherence to grammatical and structural norms. Narration should be graded based on how well the learner imitates the sentence or paragraph, whereas note taking should be graded based on how well a learner extracts pertinent information.

Should I do all the structured writing exercises in this guide?

Structured writing provides learners with a step-by-step approach to a variety of writing forms. It is divided into six sections: literary, persuasion, expository, functional, research, and narrative. If your learner progresses through a given assignment easily, you may move on to the next exercise. For instance, if your learner masters the art of writing a book report, then you can advance to a book review. The format writing order is a loose guide. It does not have to be followed stringently. However, the literary analysis and college research paper are to be done by advanced learners and should not be attempted until after your learner has mastered all of the other forms of writing.

If my learner cannot complete a book report by himself/herself, should I just move on to the next literary writing step, knowing that he/she will eventually master the book report?

No, each step builds on the other. The learner must first do the book report, then book review, then literary response paper, and finally the literary analysis.

How long should I give my learner to complete a research paper?

Research papers require at least two weeks to research, draft and execute. Review each step of the research paper writing process, and then estimate how long it will take for your learner to finish each step. Remember research and prewriting take a considerable amount of time. You should also add extra time for the learner's other activities and subjects.

This program almost seems too easy. Is it really that simple?

You should start your children journaling daily about subjects they are studying. (See writing prompts suggestions.) You should progress through the format writing section slowly. It is suggested that you work on a different form of writing each academic quarter. The functional writing section should be progressed through quickly and should serve as a refresher course.

Grammar exercises should be worked on daily. Narration and note taking, which are essentially copy and summary work, should be done once a week. You may alternate between note taking and narration weekly. If you concentrate on note taking one week, you can alternate with narration writing the next week.

Finally, structured writing or a specific type of writing should be done at least twice a week. The learner should spend at least two days working on a structured writing assignment. It may take learners a few weeks to complete a format writing assignment, especially larger projects. Few of the format writing assignments can be accomplished in one week. You should do a study plan sheet with your learner before assigning him/her a long-term paper. You should choose the rubric you want to use with each assignment and give it to your learner before he/she begins writing.

Cheryl R. Carter

Part Two

Write with Clarity

Making a thousand decisions, even the wise will make a mistake.... 智者千虑必有一失 [智者千慮必有一失] Zhìzhě qiān lǜ, bì yǒu yī shī

The Writing Process

There are five components to the writing process that all learners should know.

Step One: Prewriting

Prewriting is the most important step in writing because sufficient time spent in prewriting will shorten the time spent drafting and revising. Prewriting involves thinking and planning, arguably the two most important elements of writing. There are many ways to engage in the prewriting process, including using a graphic organizer, doing timed free writing, speaking with others to get ideas, researching, and outlining.

Step Two: Writing the Draft

If you have spent adequate time in the prewriting process, this step should come effortlessly. Most learners work from an outline or notes. When writing the rough draft, one should not stop to count words or correct grammar. Thoughts should flow freely. Make sure you have at least an hour of uninterrupted time to write your first draft.

Writing the First Draft:

> 1- Write as rapidly as you can. Do not self-edit.
> 2- You may revise your introduction or conclusion after you write your first draft.
> 3- When writing your draft, use a line or brackets to indicate that you have to return to a section. For instance, you may add research or examples to make a point.
> 4- Revise your thesis statement, if necessary.
> 5- Work from your outline or graphic organizer.

Step Three: Revising your paper

The revision process involves four distinct steps: adding material, rearranging material, removing text, and replacing material. You may add material. Ask yourself, what else does the reader need to know? If the required word count is not met, go back to prewriting (or the planning stage) and consider what else can be added to the paper. Even if a plan was followed, sections may still need to be rearranged. You may need to reorder your paragraphs to make your argument stronger. Material may need to be removed. You may need to take out material to meet the word count. Examples and extraneous stories can often be cut to meet the word count. Finally, material may need to be replaced. This may mean replacing stories as well as rewriting sentences or entire paragraphs.

Activities

Content

- Do I need to add examples or research?
- Is my thesis statement well-developed?
- Does my closing paragraph summarize or emphasize my main point?
- Is my introductory paragraph strong?
- Do I hook readers with a shocking anecdote, event, research story, question, or statistic?
- Did I use strong topic sentences/thesis statements?
- Did I vary the types of sentences (simple, complex, and compound)?
- Did I use the passive voice minimally?
- Do my sentences logically follow one another?
- Do my ideas help the reader understand the paper's content?

Organization

- Do my paragraphs transition well into one another?
- Do all the paragraphs relate to one another?
- Are the ideas logical and do they relate to the main idea of the essay?
- Are my paragraphs reasonable, with one main idea?
- Do my ideas flow logically from one to the next?
- Is my introduction exciting and inviting?

- Does each paragraph have a strong topic sentence or a thesis statement?
- Is my conclusion strong and decisive?
- Did I stay on topic?
- Does my argument or premise make sense?

Step Four: Editing

This step often takes time, because some writers agonize over every single word. Many writers find it helpful to have a checklist such as the following that addresses sentence structure, content, and organization:

Sentence Structure, Mechanics, Grammar, and Spelling

- Do my subjects and verbs agree?
- Did I spell all words correctly?
- Are there periods after every sentence?
- Are quotation marks used for dialogue?
- Are there any fragments or run-on sentences?
- Did I spell out all abbreviations?
- Did I take out all slang?
- Are my word choices correct?

Five: Publish or turn in the paper

This means the paper meets all of the standards expected of your grade level. All papers should have one-inch margins, a cover or title page, and twelve-point font. You should ensure that you meet the instructor's word count. Also, the paper should be clean.

Summary

Learners should follow the five steps of writing when approaching most writing assignments. The steps overlap and are recursive in scope, in that you cannot follow them completely in sequence. The steps do provide a framework for learners to approach more writing assignments.

Cheryl R. Carter

Writing Basics Activities for your Learner

\Write a three-paragraph essay on air pollution.

1- Set the timer for five minutes and write about what you already know about the subject.

2- Make a list of everything you know about the topic.

3-Use a graphic organizer and brainstorm about your topic. Put the main idea in the center circle.

4-Write a letter to a friend, teacher, or parent about what you are attempting to write about or what you already know about the topic.

5-Do some preliminary research on your topic. Read a book or an article.

Thesis Statements

A thesis sentence guides the entire paper. A subject plus an opinion is a thesis statement. A college thesis statement must present an argument; you cannot just provide information about your topic. For instance, a strong thesis statement might be:

> *DNA is a method used to solve crimes but some wonder about the moral implications of using DNA to solve crimes.*

In this example, the writer is not describing DNA or how it is used. Instead, the writer represents an opinion that can be argued. In this case, some could argue it has no moral implications. If the writer was simply describing DNA, no counterargument could be made, and it would not be a thesis statement.

If you ask an average beginning writer what he/she is writing about, he/she will often give you a phrase, word, or idea. For instance, he/she may say he/she is writing about electric cars. *Electric cars* is not a complete thought or main idea. *Electric cars* is a subject or a broad generalization. A thesis statement has a specific idea and a definite assertion or predicate.

It is not enough to say you are writing a paragraph about electric cars. You must make an assertion about the electric cars. In other words, *electric cars* is your subject, but you need a predicate that makes an assertion. You might discuss the dollar fuel savings of electric cars or the marketing of electric cars. Your main idea must be a complete thought or sentence.

Predicate	Declaration
Electric cars are better for the environment than gasoline cars.	*Electric cars are the wave of the future and will replace the traditional car.*

Remember: A simple declarative sentence has few words and is clear and concise.

It is in the active voice, not passive voice. It sounds authoritative.

It is open to debate. Someone can take an opposing position.

> *Electric cars are economically a better investment than traditional cars.*

Your main idea sums up all of the evidence about the subject of your writing. For instance, if you wanted to write about electric cars and found information that showed electric cars are environmentally friendly, your thesis statement might be:

> *Electric cars are better than traditional gasoline powered cars because they are environmentally friendly.*

Notice that the thesis statement is always stated in the affirmative. It is difficult to prove a negative statement. It is, therefore, essential that the topic or thesis sentence be stated in the affirmative.

A thesis statement is one simple declarative sentence with an assertion, much like the topic sentence. You must state your thesis in the present tense with an active voice. A thesis statement may be placed at the end of a paragraph. Some writers prefer to boldly declare their thesis statements at the beginning of the paragraph.

At times, your instructor may give you a question that must be turned into a thesis statement. The question is not the thesis statement. The strong declarative response to the question is the thesis statement. The thesis is the strong controlling idea that guides the reader. The thesis statement captures the purpose, intent, and tone of the essay. A thesis is a proposition supported by a logical discussion of ideas in a sentence. It is also debatable; the best thesis statements are those with some controversy.

Thesis statements should be formed carefully and have a singular purpose. Do not use more than one subject or verb, as this tends to weigh down the thesis statement, making it less effective. For instance, if your thesis statement was long like this one, it could be confusing:

> *Electric cars should replace gasoline automobiles and the government should put money into developing them because they will preserve the environment.*

Write the Perfect Research Paper

Too many subjects are introduced. A good thesis statement reveals the audience, topic, and purpose all in one simple sentence.

Find some aspect of your research that excites you. If given the choice, chose a topic that really interests you. For example, suppose your instructor assigned you a paper on the environment. The environment is the topic of the paper. You could write about the erosion of beaches if you enjoy learning about beaches. Form a strong opinion about your topic. Take a stand; do not waver on your views. Do not apologize for your views. Most teachers enjoy reading well-developed arguments. Use concrete adjectives; do not use general words such as *good* or *bad*. For instance, do not say: *Excessive television viewing is bad.* Instead, say: *Excessive television viewing dulls the senses.*

Be sure to keep your thesis statement focused on one main idea. It should be narrow enough to be interesting but broad enough to be expanded upon in a paper. Do not write about *the failure of the school system*, because that is too broad. You can, on the other hand, write about the failure of the school system to educate special-needs learners. Be specific. Do not write: *World War II was fought for many good reasons.* Instead, say: *World War II was a moral and pragmatic war that was fought to protect our interests at home and abroad.*

Once the thesis statement is written, spend some time brainstorming ways to defend your position. Jot down points to defend the thesis statement, or use a graphic organizer. Your research will then be directed by the points that will prove your thesis statement. On the other hand, some prefer to research first and then form a thesis statement based on the amount of research available on a subject. Thesis statements on familiar topics are easy to write and then research, whereas unfamiliar topics may demand substantial background research before the thesis statement can be formed.

What is a thesis statement?

> - A thesis statement must be debatable or controversial.
> - Ask yourself, would an organized group, association, organization, or ethnic group agree or disagree with your thesis statement? Can you offer an effective counterargument?
> - Is it specific? Do you target a specific book, group, time period, geographic location, person, organization, etc.? The more specific your thesis statement, the better.
> - Does it take a position? The position should be in the affirmative. It is difficult to argue the negative.
> - Is the thesis statement shocking or impacting? Does it cause your reader to think? Does it surprise you?
> - Is your thesis statement in your first paragraph? Is it affirmed in your final paragraph?

A strong thesis statement is critical to a strong paper. It is important to note that a thesis statement is not a question, nor is it a statement of purpose or a topic. The following do not make good thesis statements.

Example A: *The purpose of this paper is to look at the budget crisis.*

This is a statement of purpose, not a thesis statement. It tells what you will write the paper about but does not take a position. The following is a thesis statement: *The budget crisis has caused massive layoffs and disrupted millions of families in the Silicon Valley and could have easily been prevented if funds had been managed correctly.*

Example B: *Why are there so many gangs in Waschovis?*

This is a question. A question can never be a thesis statement. You may answer the question and take a position to transform it into a strong thesis statement. The following is a thesis statement: *Gangs in Waschovis have terrorized the area for such a long time, and the reason for their existence is clear: the breakdown of the family in that area.*

> **Example C:** *The educational system in New York City is interesting.*

This is not a thesis statement. This is a topic. No position is taken. The following is a thesis statement: *The educational system in New York City was designed to socialize new immigrants and to prepare them for jobs in the New World; it was not designed to educate children and little has changed over the years.*

Summary

A thesis statement guides your paper. It should be strong, focused, and specific. It is the foundation of any good paper. Significant time should be spent developing a strong thesis statement. The thesis statement should state the reason or purpose of your paper, and your opinion should be firmly stated.

Cheryl R. Carter

Thesis Student Worksheet

Indicate whether the sentence is an effective thesis statement. Tell why or why not.

1-*Cars alone do not cause pollution.*

.

2-*The hockey game was fun.*

3-*Othello is an interesting character.*

4-*Business administration offers many opportunities for college graduates.*

5-*Shakespeare should be necessary reading for all high school learners.*

.

6-*The automobile industry has spurred an increase in air pollution in the greater Chicago area.*

7-*Tall people are employed by companies with high ceilings and huge financial input.*

8-*Western philosophy supports all Christian religious practices.*

.

9-*In this paper, I will prove colicky babies cry a long time.*

.

10-*The White House is elegantly decorated during the holiday season.*

Part II

Write the Perfect Research Paper

Make these stronger thesis statements:

Why should the president of the United States serve more than one term?

The solar system is in the sky.

This paper will look at the different kinds of coins.

Cheryl R. Carter

Thesis Statement Activities Worksheet

Indicate whether the sentence is an effective thesis statement. Tell why or why not.

1-*Cars alone do not cause pollution.*

No. It is difficult to prove the negative. It would be better to say, *Buses and cars cause air pollution.*

2-*The hockey game was fun.*

No. This is a general statement. It is not debatable or powerful.

3-*Othello is an interesting character.*

No. It is too general and not controversial.

4-*Business administration offers many opportunities for college graduates.*

No. It is too general and not debatable or impacting.

5-*Shakespeare should be necessary reading for all high school learners.*

Yes. It is controversial, takes a position, and some educators might disagree with the statement.

6-*The automobile industry has spurred an increase in air pollution in the greater Chicago area.*

Yes. It cites a specific problem in a specific geographic area.

7-*Tall people are employed by companies with high ceilings and huge financial input.*

Yes. It is a shocking statement that must be proven.

8-*Western philosophy supports all Christian religious practices.*

Yes. It is specific and debatable.

9-*In this paper, I will prove colicky babies cry a long time.*

No. This is an accepted fact. It is not shocking or controversial. Few people would disagree with this statement.

10-*The White House is elegantly decorated during the holiday season.*

No. This is not shocking. It is a general statement.

Part II

Make these stronger thesis statements:

Why should the president of the United States serve more than one term?

Answers will vary. The responses should be specific and take a position. The question should be transformed into a question.

The solar system is in the sky.

Answer may vary. This is a topic. It is not a thesis sentence.

This paper will look at the different kinds of coins.

Answer may vary. This is a statement of purpose. The response should state something about the topic.

Cheryl R. Carter

Structuring Paragraphs

There are primarily three kinds of paragraphs: introductory, concluding, and the body paragraph.

A body paragraph contains the supporting ideas or evidence to prove your thesis correct. These paragraphs usually begin with a topic sentence. Use the active voice to build your argument. The active voice speaks with authority. You may also quote in your paragraph to gain credibility. For instance, you might say: *Electric cars are the hottest talk in automobile boardrooms, according to Grant Frank, president of United Automobiles.*

Most body paragraphs will summarize information or evidence. Body paragraphs help the reader to make connections with the material and to understand the material in context. You should always have at least three supporting points in each paragraph to keep the paragraphs meaty and vibrant. If you have fewer than three supporting facts, your paragraph will be sparse.

If your paragraphs are too sparse, you may build them in three ways: (1) You may use a story or an anecdote to illustrate a point. (2) You may use an analogy where you take something that the reader is familiar with and connect it to a new idea. Analogies describe and explain. (3) You may provide concrete examples.

Your introductory paragraph must get the reader's attention with an astounding fact, intriguing question, or outlandish statement. This is referred to as the "hook." Your introduction also sets the tone for the essay and defines and provides background information for the reader. State your thesis at the end of the paragraph once you have laid the foundation for the reader.

An introductory paragraph is like a triangle. The information moves from the broad to the specific. For instance, the paragraph may discuss the dangers of drug abuse, but then the topic is narrowed down to the specifics of prescription drug abuse.

The introductory paragraph of a research paper often does not contain any supporting facts for the thesis. It may be tempting to address the thesis with supporting facts in the introductory paragraph, but this would not serve the essay overall.

Write the Perfect Research Paper

First Paragraph Hooks

> Quotation: *Schools were designed to socialize immigrants and to reduce the crime rate, according to the U.S. Secretary of Education.*
>
> Humor: *Lisa decided it was best to wear red for St. Patrick's Day after all she had dyed the entire laundry red by mistake.*
>
> Shocking Fact: *Schools graduate less than half the learners who enroll yearly. Of those that do graduate, less than half of them are prepared for college level work.*
>
> Anecdote: *After cleaning out the gutters, Ray realized he had forgotten to properly dispose of the old leaves. The back yard was strewn with dead leaves. Now an even bigger task awaited him.*
>
> Peak interest: *Most people think that dogs are the most loyal animals but rabbits are really man's best friend.*
>
> Question: *Have you ever wondered how we dispose of all our trash and waste products?*
>
> Statistic: *Seventy percent of all children learning to count cannot remember the number thirteen.*

Your concluding paragraph generally picks up ideas that were used in the introduction. You may recap the main ideas, stating them a bit differently than you did in the body paragraphs. In many essays, the concluding paragraph may be very brief.

Ways to Conclude Paragraphs

> Summarize ideas: *In conclusion, the traffic pattern can best be rectified according to the research by adding another on-ramp to the interstate.*

Anecdote that makes your point: *Sammy looked at me and pouted just as he had seen the characters on television do. He insisted television had no effect on him.*

Question that suggests further research or thought: *Can we ever resolve the issue of homelessness given the complexity of the problem?*

Best part of your research: *By far the most convincing part of this study showed that ninety percent of divorced couples said they never would have married if they had received mandatory premarital counseling.*

Paragraphs must have a clear, logical train of thought so transitions can occur naturally. Transitioning takes planning (see suggested transitional words under note taking). As an individual grows as a writer, he will find he can connect sentences almost unconsciously because sentences naturally build on one another.

Quick review: A paragraph should always have a topic sentence and at least four supporting sentences. A paragraph's length may vary, but in academic writing you should aim for a minimum of four sentences that support your topic sentence. The last sentence of your paragraph should be a closing or transitional sentence. A transitional sentence leads the reader to the next paragraph. You might state something like, *Next we will discuss...* (insert your topic). Here is a list of transitional words to begin a new paragraph:

To continue a common line of reasoning:
- consequently
- clearly, then
- furthermore
- additionally
- and
- in addition
- moreover
- because
- besides that
- also
- following this further

- in the same way
- pursuing this further
- in light of the…it is easy to see that

To change the line of reasoning (contrast):
- however
- on the other hand
- but
- yet
- nevertheless
- on the contrary

For opening a paragraph initially or for general use:
- admittedly
- assuredly
- certainly
- granted
- no doubt
- at this level
- obviously
- of course
- to be sure
- truly
- undoubtedly
- generally speaking
- unquestionably
- nobody denies
- in this situation
- in general

For the final points of a paragraph or essay:
- finally
- lastly

Transitional chains, to use in separating sections of a paragraph which is arranged chronologically:
- basically
- similarly
- as well
- to be sure
- lastly
- additionally
- generally
- furthermore
- finally
- also
- in the first place
- just in the same way
- in the first place
- pursuing this further
- first…second…third…

To signal conclusion:
- therefore
- thus
- hence
- indeed
- in conclusion
- in final analysis
- in final consideration

To restate a point within a paragraph in another way or in a more exacting way:
- in other words
- point in fact
- specifically

Sequence or time

- after
- afterward
- as soon as
- at first
- at last
- before
- before long
- finally
- first…second…third
- in the first place
- in the meantime
- later
- meanwhile
- next
- soon
- then

Summary

There are three kinds of paragraphs: the introduction, the conclusion, and the body paragraph. A paragraph should be focused on one main point. Generally, but not always, the first sentence of a paragraph should be a topic sentence, except in the case of introductory and concluding paragraphs. These types of paragraphs begin differently because they have to grab the reader's attention, whereas body paragraphs simply transition between ideas.

Cheryl R. Carter

Paragraph Student Worksheet

Write four supporting statements and a concluding or transitional sentence for at least two of the topic sentences below.

The automobile industry is important to the United States economy.

Modern missionaries must be adept at using technology.

The fall season is a great a time to set goals.

The expression "time is money" is accurate.

Contrary to popular belief, the atom is not the smallest particle in the universe.

The Declaration of Independence marked a turning point in the way the colonists were governed.

Part II

Indicate whether each sentence is a good way to begin a paragraph.

1- *Terry and Molly came along for the ride to the museum.*

2- *Eight out of ten teenagers believe their parents' financial advice is worth adhering to on a regular basis.*

3- *Business management is an excellent career path.*

4- *Burritos taste good. Mexico is a friendly country.*

5- *Should Americans participate in a national consumer organization?*

6-*The day Aunt Franny came to visit was so eventful.*

7-*Finally, if the sheriff wants to release the funds for the new jail, then he should consider the cost to the taxpayer.*

8-*Jerry Lewis is a funny comedian.*

9-*Eagles' wings help them to fly.*

Cheryl R. Carter

Student Paragraph Answer Sheet:

Write four supporting statements and a concluding or transitional sentence for at least two of the topic sentences below.

The automobile industry is important to the United States economy.

Modern missionaries must be adept at using technology.

The fall season is a great a time to set goals.

The expression "time is money" is accurate.

Contrary to popular belief, the atom is not the smallest particle in the universe.

The Declaration of Independence marked a turning point in the way the colonists were governed.

Part II

Indicate whether each sentence is a good way to begin a paragraph.

1-*Terry and Molly came along for the ride to the museum.*

No. If you are writing an essay, you need to be specific and let the reader know what you are writing about.

2-*Eight out of ten teenagers believe their parents' financial advice is worth adhering to on a regular basis.*

Yes, because it is shocking.

3-*Business management is an excellent career path.*

Yes. It introduces the subject.

4-*Burritos taste good. Mexico is a friendly country.*

No, because these sentences do not tell you what the paragraph will be about.

5-*Should Americans participate in a national consumer organization?*

Yes. This is an interesting question.

6-*The day Aunt Franny came to visit was so eventful.*

Yes. It uses a story.

7-*Finally, if the sheriff wants to release the funds for the new jail, then he should consider the cost to the taxpayer.*

Yes. It summarizes a topic and is likely a concluding paragraph.

8-*Jerry Lewis is a funny comedian.*

Yes, it tells the reader what he/she is going to be reading about in the paragraph.

9-*Eagles' wings help them to fly.*

No, unless the paragraph is just about eagles' wings. If it is about eagles in general, it is not a good sentence.

Cheryl R. Carter

Taking Notes for Stronger Arguments

Taking notes is the first step in thinking critically about the material. It is not enough to just read through articles, books, journals, etc. Eventually, the information has to be molded into a persuasive or informative, cohesive form. When learners take notes, they are thinking on their own and taking the material to a different level by putting it in a form that can be used differently than the author intended. In essence, the learner produces a completely new work based on his ability to assimilate the material, whereas in narration the learner merely summarizes or sequences events or ideas logically. Note taking does involve a certain amount of summarization and critical assimilation of the material.

Step One: Find the main idea

The learner should ask, what was the main idea or main point of the literary work? Or, to put it another way, the learner should ask, why did the author write the material? The main idea is the major point of the story, chapter, or text. If the main idea is not obvious, look at the title, chapter, or heading of the book. This will often reveal the main idea. Often the main idea of a paragraph is the topic sentence, which generally appears as the first sentence in a paragraph.

As you read, underline any unknown vocabulary that seems related to the topic. You can use Post-it notes if you are using a library book or a book that will be used by a sibling. Often, the main idea is not stated specifically but is suggested through examples and stories. Stories and examples often amplify the main idea. If you are in doubt about the main idea, look for examples and illustrations, as these often make the main idea clearer.

Step Two: Summarize your note

Depending on the length of the article, chapter, or story you are summarizing, list at least three points. Generally, it is easy to do this if you find the main idea or topic sentence from each paragraph. Ask yourself, do I understand each point and how does it relate to the main idea? In your own words, jot down how you think it relates to the main idea. It is important to use your own words to cement your understanding of a concept. If you cannot discuss a concept, idea, or fact in your own words, then you probably do not understand it.

Write the Perfect Research Paper

You can also summarize by getting rid of extraneous words by removing examples, illustrations, references to studies, anecdotes, and stories that do not pertain to the main point. Repeated words or redundant words can also be eliminated. Generally, the first and last paragraphs have most of the key points in them. Pay close attention to the first and last paragraphs, because these paragraphs generally summarize the content.

Step Three: Organize your points

After you brainstorm the main points of a book, chapter, or article, write the ideas down in full sentences. Place a 1, 2, 3, etc., near what you think are the strongest or most important points, with 1 indicating the most important point or fact and 2 being the next and descending. Ask yourself if you can remove any point or fact, especially if it is an example or repeats another fact.

Step Four: Write a topic sentence

After you have written all of the points in summary, write a topic sentence that encompasses the main idea. Then, write a brief paragraph that joins each sentence together smoothly. One way to do this is by using transitions—words or phrases or techniques that help bring two ideas together. Certain words help continue an idea, indicate a shift of thought or contrast, or sum up a conclusion.

Step Five: Clarify your note

Read your summary aloud and ask yourself, is there anything that is not clear? Review the first four steps.

Step Six: Record the notes on index cards

Write the note on an index card. In the upper left-hand corner, write the topic of the paper. On the right side of the paper, write the author, title, and page number. Write the note in the center of the index card. Only one summary note should be on each card.

Example:

Self-Reliance, by Ralph Waldo Emerson

There is a time in every man's education when he arrives at the conviction that envy is ignorance; that imitation is suicide; that he must take himself for better, for worse, as his portion; that though the wide universe is full of good, no kernel of nourishing corn can come to him but through his toil bestowed on that plot of ground which is given to him to till. The power which resides in him is new in nature, and none but he knows what that is which he can do, nor does he know until he has tried. Not for nothing one face, one character, one fact, makes much impression on him, and another none. This sculpture in the memory is not without preestablished harmony. The eye was placed where one ray should fall, that it might testify of that particular ray. We but half express ourselves, and are ashamed of that divine idea which each of us represents. It may be safely trusted as proportionate and of good issues, so it be faithfully imparted, but God will not have his work made manifest by cowards. A man is relieved and gay when he has put his heart into his work and done his best; but what he has said or done otherwise, shall give him no peace. It is a deliverance which does not deliver. In the attempt his genius deserts him; no muse befriends; no invention, no hope.

Summary Note:

An individual must not compare himself/herself to another if he/she is to be successful. One should attempt new tasks with confidence that they can be done in his/her own ability or inner strength. An individual can only be proud of what he/she accomplishes on his/her own without comparison or compromise.

Write the Perfect Research Paper

Note Card

```
Literary topic or          Author
question
                           Title

                           Page #


        Fact, thought, quote, or
             note summary
```

Further Instructions on Summary Notes

There is not one definitive way to summarize. Practice helps develop this skill. When approaching a portion of text, some find the following steps help them to summarize thoughts, ideas, or concepts:

1- Strike a line through the material that is not important to the understanding of the material.
2- Strike a line through words or phrases that repeat information.
3- Replace one word with a group of items; for example, football, soccer, baseball, etc., might be replaced with the word *sports*.
4- Circle the topic sentence. The topic sentence will help you form the summary.

Asking questions also helps us to summarize. Questions help us to frame our summaries because they point us in the correct direction and force us to focus on the main idea.

Here are some questions based on the genre (or type of writing) to ask when composing a summary note:

Fiction or Narrative Essay

- Who are the main characters, and what distinguishes them from others?
- When and where did the story take place? What were the circumstances?
- What prompted the action in the story?
- How did the characters express their feelings?
- What did the main characters decide to do? Did they set a goal, and, if so, what was it?
- How did the main characters try to accomplish their goal(s)?
- What were the consequences?

Opinion or Argumentative Essay

- What information is presented that leads to the claim?
- What is the basic statement or claim that is the focus of the information?
- What examples, facts, or other evidence are presented to support this claim?
- What concessions are made about the claim?

Definition

- What concept is being defined?
- To which general category does the item belong?
- What are the attributes or characteristics of this concept?
- What examples are given to illustrate this concept?

Compare or Contrast

- What is being compared?
- What are the characteristics that form the basis of the comparison?
- What do these items have in common?

- How are they different?
- What conclusions does the author draw about the comparison?

Problem-Solution

- What is the problem?
- What is a possible solution?
- What is another possible solution?
- Which solution has the best chance of succeeding?

Chronological

- What event or sequence of events is being described?
- Who are the people who play a role in this event(s)?
- Where does the event(s) occur?
- In what order do the major incidences occur?
- What caused this event and what happens as a result of it?

Cause/Effect and Process

- What is the process or topic being explained?
- What are the steps in the process or causal events that occur?
- What is the outcome of the process or causal events?

Paraphrase notes

Paraphrasing notes takes a great deal of practice. This type of note is generally used in research paper writing. Never use the same sentence structure as the original words or text. When paraphrasing you must capture the main ideas of the author, but you do not necessarily use the exact words.

A paraphrase can be as long as the original, whereas a summary note consolidates the information. A paraphrase does not rely on quotes and simply attempts to capture the writer's main idea. A paraphrase is not set within quotation marks because it should be a synthesis of your ideas and the author's. The paraphrase should still be cited because it is not your ideas. A paraphrase does not use the same words or structure.

A paraphrased note expresses an author's ideas in your own words. This type of note is best used in your conclusion or the summary portion of your paper. This shows your instructor you understand what you are writing about. For instance, you might say after reading about John Hancock, a signer of the Declaration of Independence, that he understood *freedom would come at any cost.* He never actually said that but these words represent a paraphrase of his ideas. The steps to do this are rather simple.

Step One: Read the material carefully

Read over the chapter, paragraph, or article a few times, then close the book. Turn or fold the page so that you are not tempted to glance at it again. Jot down notes from the source that you remember. Unlike summary notes, you are encouraged when paraphrasing to use the same vocabulary of the original source. Write down what you think is the main idea.

Step Two: Write what you think is the essence of the original

Write what you think is the essence of the original. Return to the original. Read it again to see if you have the general sense of the original piece. Add or remove any points that do not accurately reflect the main idea.

Step Three: Review what you have written
Reread your paraphrased writing; ask yourself if it makes sense. Does it have the same intent as the original? A paraphrase is subjective. No two paraphrases are exactly the same. The following example is just a guide.

Example:

The immune system protects our bodies from disease. Cells called *white blood cells* found in our blood are able to kill bad things, such as bacteria and virus.

There are many different types of white blood cells. Some of them make things called antibodies that stick to things that enter our bodies, making these substances easy to find. Other white blood cells get rid of bacteria and stop viruses like the flu.

When our immune system does not work well, we are vulnerable to disease caused by bacteria and virus. Problems with the immune system include allergies; in allergies, white blood cells attack things that are not bad, like pollen in our eyes or cat dander.

Paraphrased:

Our bodies need protection from disease to live and thrive. Our immune system performs this function. White blood cells destroy disease-prone substances in our blood. There are different types of white blood cells. Some make antibodies that adhere to substances in our bodies and are easily detectable. Other blood cells keep bacteria out as well as fight viruses. Allergies occur when our immune system attacks substances that are not harmful in our body, such as pollen in our eyes or cat dander.

Note Card:

```
┌─────────────────────────────────────────┐
│                                         │
│   Research topic           Author       │
│   or question                           │
│                            Title        │
│                                         │
│                            Page #       │
│                                         │
│                                         │
│          Fact, thought, quote, or       │
│             note summary                │
│                                         │
└─────────────────────────────────────────┘
```

Quotation Notes

Quotation notes are used to hammer home a point because this type of note brings authority to research. This note uses the exact words of the author. For instance, you might say: *Patrick Henry believed in freedom. He said, "Give me liberty or give me death."*

Step One: Choose a quote.

Chose a quote and personally reflect on the words. What do you think the author meant? Why do you think he/she said it? The quote should stand out and be a bit controversial or shocking.

Write the Perfect Research Paper

Step Two: Write your reflections.

Read the quote again and write down your first impression of the quote. Explain why the quote appealed to you.

Step Three: Choose how you will use the quote in your paper.

Determine precisely how you will use the quote. Will it be used to verify a point you want to make? Will it be used to dismiss the opposing view or opinion? Quotes should be used purposefully in your papers.

Example:

Henry Ford said, "All entrepreneurs must want to succeed." It is true that people must want to achieve their goals.

Note Card:

```
┌─────────────────────────────────────────────────┐
│                                                 │
│   It is true that people must        Henry Ford │
│   want to achieve their goals?                  │
│                                                 │
│                                                 │
│       "All entrepreneurs must want to succeed." │
│                                                 │
└─────────────────────────────────────────────────┘
```

Cheryl R. Carter

Notes Student Worksheet

Comment on these quotes:

1-"Believe you can and you are halfway there."—Theodore Roosevelt

2-"Don't judge each day by the harvest you reap but by the seeds that you plant."—Robert Louis Stevenson

3-"God always gives His best to those who leave the choice with him."—Jim Elliot

4-"How wonderful it is that nobody need wait a single moment before starting to improve the world."—Anne Frank

5-"Once you learn to read you are forever free."—Frederick Douglass

Part II

Paraphrase and/or summarize a paragraph from your history, science, computer, etc., textbook.

Summarize a passage using the following steps:

Strike a line through the material that is not important to the understanding of the material.

Strike a line through words or phrases that repeat information.

Replace one word with a group of items; for example, football, soccer, baseball, etc., might be replaced with the word sports.

Circle the topic sentence.

Summarize a work of fiction by answering the following questions:

Who are the main characters, and what distinguishes them from others?

When and where did the story take place? What were the circumstances?

What prompted the action in the story?

How did the characters express their feelings?

What did the main characters decide to do? Did they set a goal, and, if so, what was it?

How did the main characters try to accomplish their goal(s)?

What were the consequences?

Cheryl R. Carter

Citations in Your Writing

After you have composed your thesis and taken notes, it is time to write your outline. You begin this process by asking yourself, what is the purpose of my paper? Why does my instructor want me to write the paper? Your paper must have a cohesive structure that clearly represents each idea. A well-developed outline ensures that your paper has direction and structure.

Your outline may consist of the main points of each paragraph, or you may use questions that you want to answer. You may assign a paragraph for each question. The question method is quite effective when writing a lengthy research paper. Remember, your thesis statement should be in your introductory paragraph.

Citations that appear in your paper are called in-text citations. All research papers contain information from other sources. When you use information that has been previously published by someone else, it is important that you avoid plagiarism—presenting someone else's ideas as your own. Plagiarism is stealing someone else's ideas. You can include someone else's ideas in your paper by putting those ideas into your own words or quoting them directly.

Modern Language Association (MLA) and American Psychological Association (APA) styles are being revised, and therefore you are encouraged to visit their Web sites. Visit www. Apastyle.org and www. MLA.org.

APA

Quote

In APA, if your quote is less than forty words, you may simply put quotation marks around it and include it with the rest of the paragraph after you have cited the source of the quote. If you quote more than forty words, then it's a block quote. In this case, do not use quotation marks; instead start the quote on a new line and indent one-half inch. Always introduce a block quote.

Write the Perfect Research Paper

Paraphrase

Lawrence loved power so much that he actually committed murder in order to inherit the position. (Luxley, 2005).

Quote from a Source with Page Numbers

At least one study has shown that "the genetic mutations of the ant also affect the spider" (Ortiz-Counterman, & Noor, 2004, p. 37).

Quote from a Source with No Page Numbers

As Gibbs & Smith have stated, "an influenza pandemic, by definition, occurs only when the influenza virus mutates into something dangerously unfamiliar to our immune systems and yet is able to jump from person to person through a sneeze, cough, or touch" (2007).

Quote from a Source with No Page Numbers and No Author Listed

The logging of forest biomes has resulted in "hundreds of species of plants and animals disappearing from the planet on a daily basis" (Forest biomes, 2002).

Source with an Organization as Author

"Traumatic brain injury (TBI)...occurs when a sudden trauma causes damage to the brain" (National Institute ofNeurological Disorders and Stroke [NINDS], 2005).

Personal Communication

Dr. J. R. Thompson of the University of Tennessee confirmed by e-mail that superconductors have tremendous potential for saving energy by improving the electrical systems (personal communication, September 3, 2011).

Reference Page

Book

Author. (Year). *Book title* (edition). City: Publisher.
Morrison, T. (1998). *Paradise.* New York: Alfred A. Knopf.

Book (No Author Listed)

Book title (edition). (Year). City: Publisher.

Publication manual of the American Psychological Association (5th ed.). (2001). Washington, DC: American Psychological Association.

Journal Article

Author. (Year). Article title. *Journal Title. Volume* (Issue), Pages.

Luxner, L. (2005). Famous footsteps of a stadium. *Americas*, 57 (5), 4-5.

Section in a Book (Article, Essay, Chapter, etc.)

Author. (Year). Article or chapter title. In Editor Name (Ed.), *Book title* (Volume, pages). City:Publisher.

Lucas, W. (2001). Search engines, relevancy, and the world wide web. In A.G. Chin (Ed.), *Textdatabases and document management: Theory and practice* (pp. 22-51). Hershey, PA: Idea Group Publishing.

Page Article/Book from Database

Gibbs, W., & Soares, C. (2005). Preparing for a pandemic. *Scientific American*, 293(5), 44-54. Retrieved October 20, 2005, from the Academic Search Premier database. Kaye, P. (2005). Learning. *The New Book of Knowledge*. Scholastic Library Publishing. Retrieved October 24, 2005, from the Grolier Online database.

MLA

In MLA style, if the quoted text is more than four lines, you should put it in a separate paragraph (without quotation marks) and indent it by one inch. Either way, you should introduce the quotation and make sure to explain how the information relates to your paper.

Book or Article with an Author

The land mines were placed by the overt government to kill and maim the warriors (Arnold 45-46).

Book or Article (Author Mentioned in Text)
Arnold states that tourism, encouraged by the government, is one of Greece's largest industries (45-46).

Book or Article (Two Authors)
Picasso's attraction to art came at an early age; in fact, he "was able to draw before he could speak, and he could speak long before he was able to walk" (Bernadac and Bouchet 19).

Article in a Multivolume Reference Book
The abundance of natural resources in Great Britain and its colonies was one factor that allowed the Industrial Revolution to begin there (Emerson 10:248).

Article in a Multivolume Reference Book (No Author)
Globally, no other infectious disease kills more people than tuberculosis ("Tuberculosis" 3:875).

Online Source (No Page Numbers)
Studies show the most enduring social movements have been started by Christians (Naylor).

Online Source (No Author or Page Numbers)
Available as a free download, OpenOffice is a popular open source alternative to Microsoft Office ("OpenOffice 3.0").

Works Cited Page

Book (Print)
Author. Title of Book. City of Publication: Publisher, Year. Format.
Arnold, Francis. Greece. Austin: Steck-Vaughn, 1992. Print.

Bernadac, Marie-Laure, and Paule Bouchet. Picasso: Master of the New Idea. New York: Abrams, 1993. Print.
E-book (from a database).

Author. Title of Book. City of Publication: Publisher, Year. Database Title. Format. Date of Access.

Katz, Mark. Capturing Sound: How Technology Has Changed Music. Berkley: U of California P, 2004. netLibrary. Web. 15 Feb. 2006.
Article in a Reference Book or Edited Collection (Print)
Author. "Title of Article." Title of Book. Editor. Volume. City of Publication: Publisher, Year. Pages. Format.

Bewley, Marius. "The True Heir of the American Dream." Readings on *The Great Gatsby*. Ed. Katie de Koster. San Diego: Greenhaven, 1998. 96-103. Print.

Lampard, Eric Edwin. "Industrial Revolution." World Book Encyclopedia. Vol. 10. Chicago: World Book, 2000. 246-255. Print.
"Tuberculosis." Human Diseases and Conditions. Ed. Neil Izenberg. Vol. 3. New York: Scribner's, 2000. 875-880. Print.

Reference or Encyclopedia Article (from a database)
Author. "Title of Article." Title of Book. Editor. Volume. City of Publication: Publisher, Year. Database Title. Format. Date of Access.

Rickards, Joseph. "Photorealism." Encyclopedia Americana. 2009. Grolier Online. Web. 21 Oct. 2009.

Henningfeld, Diane. "Overview of The Bluest Eye." EXPLORING Novels. Detroit: Gale, 2003. Learner Resource Center – Gold. Web. 21 Oct. 2009.

Magazine or Newspaper Article (Print)
Author. "Title of Article." Magazine or Newspaper Date: Pages. Format.

Johnston, Richard. "Martin History Revisited." *Acoustic Guitar* July 2009: 60-69. Print.

Magazine or Newspaper Article (from a database)
Author. "Title of Article." Magazine or Newspaper Date: Pages. Database Title. Format. Date of Access.

Faure, Gaelle. "Managing Your Online Afterlife." *Time* 14 Sep. 2009: 51-52. MAS Ultra - School Edition. Web. 21 Oct. 2009.

Academic Journal Article (from a database)

Author. "Title of Article." Journal Title Volume.Issue (Year): Pages. Database Title. Format. Date of Access.

Matula, Theodore. "Pow! to the People: The Make-Up's Reorganization of Punk Rhetoric." *Popular Music & Society* 30.1 (2007): 19-38. Academic Search Complete. Web. 27 Oct. 2009.

Web Page
Author. "Title of Page." Title of Web Site. Publisher or Sponsor, Date of Publication. Format. Date of Access.

"Adderall." PDRhealth. PDR Network, 2009. Web. 21 Oct. 2009.

Naylor, Stephen. "Hindu Mythology." Encyclopedia Mythica. N.p., 8 Apr. 2006. Web. 21 Oct. 2009.

"OpenOffice 3.0." Osalt.com. N.p., n.d. Web. 6 Nov. 2009

Online Photograph, Illustration, or Image

Artist. Image Title. Date of Publication. Collection or Institution.

Web site or database. Format. Date of Access.

Adams, Ansel. Guayle Field, Manzanar Relocation Center. 1943.

Library of Congress. American Memory. Web. 27 Oct. 2009.

Song or Sound Recording (from a CD or MP3)

Specific Contributor. "Song Title." Other Major Contributors. Album

Title. Publisher, Year. Format.

Copeland, Aaron. "Fanfare for the Common Man." Perf. New York

Philharmonic. Cond. Leonard Bernstein. Sing America. Warner

Bros., 1999. CD.

Jimi Hendrix Experience. "All Along the Watchtower." By Bob

Dylan. Electric Ladyland. MCA, 1968. MP3.

Video or Movie (on DVD or VHS)

Specific Contributor. Title. Other Major Contributors. Distributor,

Year. Format.

Brando, Marlon, perf. A Streetcar Named Desire. By Tennessee

Williams. Dir. Elia Kazan. Warner Bros., 2006. DVD.

Video or Movie (Online)

Specific Contributor. Title. Other Major Contributors. Publisher or

Distributor, Year. Web site or database. Format. Date of Access.

Ivers, Louise, narr. Haiti: Malnutrition. Harvard University, 2009.

Works Cited Page

Author/Editor: If no author or editor, begin with the title.
1. Begin with the last name, followed by a comma and the first name. If a middle name or initial is
given, place it after the first name and add a period [Robinson, Andrea C.].
2. If a junior/senior, abbreviate, place after the last name and a comma, and follow with a period, a
Comma, and the first name [Cole, Jr., Tom].
3. If two or three authors, give the last name and first name of the first author followed by a comma
and the word *and*. Next, give the first and last name(s) of the other(s), separating him/her (them)
with a comma [Mann, Jeff, Charlie Ziegler, and Margaret A. Nelson].
4. If more than three authors, give the last name and first name of the first author followed by a comma
and *et al.* (*et al.* means *and others*) [Dudley, William, et al.].
5. If an editor instead of an author, give the last name and first name followed by a comma and the
abbreviation for *editor* (*ed.*) or *editors* (*eds.*) [Stokes, Alan, ed.], [Hill, Laura, and Dave Roe, eds.].
6. Omit a title or degree with a name [Rev. John Smith; Tong Thao, PhD].
B. Publisher (See "Publishers' Names" in *MLA Handbook*, pages 272–74, for a listing):
1. Omit the introductory articles *A, An, The*.
2. Omit business abbreviations such as *Co., Corp., Ltd.,* or *Inc.* [Anderson, Inc.].
3. Omit descriptive words such as *Books, House, Publishers, Press* [Random House].
4. Omit the first name of one-name publishers [W.W. Norton].
5. Give only the first person of multiname publishers [Little, Brown, and Smith].
6. When citing a university press, always add the abbreviation *P* [Ohio State UP].

C. City of Publication:

1. If several cities are listed, give only the first city.

2. If a city is unfamiliar, also give the state or country. Use the two-letter capitalized abbreviation for states [WI, IL, CT, NY, CA, etc.]. (See *MLA Handbook,*

Citations in Your Writing Student Worksheet

MLA

Write a Work Cited page for the following three sources:

Book with author

Web site

Reference book

Interview

APA

Write a Work Cited page for the following three sources:

Book with author

Web site

Reference book

Interview

Cheryl R. Carter

Argumentative Writing

Argumentative essays have some basic features that you should include in your essay. Argument is a key component of college writing. In general, argumentative essays require you to support the argument you are making using logic and support from your research.

Include in your argumentative essay a thesis statement that makes a clear declaration that establishes the argument. Take a solid position when writing your paper. Remember, your thesis should be in your first paragraph. Generally the thesis statement is the last sentence of your introduction paragraph. Your argumentative thesis should provide

- logical transitions that connect paragraphs and sentences
- claims that help prove your overall argument
- support for your claims from your research sources
- a conclusion that considers the evidence you have presented
- in-text citations throughout your essay to indicate where you have used sources
- a works cited page with an entry for each of your sources. Most first year college learners will use MLA in composition class, however, learners studying the social sciences will likely use APA. I strongly suggest using MLA since it will likely be used in freshman composition.

Nearly all argumentative papers employ the rhetorical devices of ethos, pathos and logos. No matter what kind of paper you write all of these elements will be a part of your essay. When all three elements of these rhetorical devices are used in an essay, the writing is very strong. Learners should aim to include each of these rhetorical devices in their writing.

Ethos relates to the ethical appeal of your writing and your credibility. Even though a topic may seem to lack ethics this is generally not true. You must make a strong ethical appeal in your essay or paper. You must also convince your readers that your argument is valid and that your arguments are weighty and worth considering. You can achieve these objectives by avoiding vague noncommittal statements, and presenting information in an unbiased manner.

Pathos refers to the emotional appeals of an argument. The emotional appeal should not be sentimental but rather more broad based with general overarching themes such as fairness, freedom, love, or human worth. Make sure that your use of emotional appeals is minimal and appropriate. Do not reference inappropriate personal examples. Appeal to general feelings of kindness or universally accepted societal norms such as sowing and reaping or the beauty of forgiveness.

Logos refers to your use of logic. Use logic to strengthen your argument. Organize your points in a way that convinces the reader your argument is solid.. You may organize your points chronologically, by cause and effect, or problem and solution. Use the outlines in *Write to Achieve* to help you make your essay stronger.

Be careful not to jump straight in your paper. Take the time to explore your thoughts on a subject by brainstorming or participating in prewriting activities. This can be done by using graphic organizers, making lists or doing timed free writing sessions. Timed free writing can be done by setting your alarm for fifteen minutes and then write down all your thoughts on your topic.

You may also just write a bulleted list of the key issues on your topic. This will help you greatly when you begin to research your topic. It also helps to write questions about your topic on a piece of paper and answer the questions. On a piece of paper, write out "Who? What? When? Where? Why? How?" Space the questions about two or three lines apart on the paper so that you can write your answers

Make sure your thesis is arguable. Review the thesis statement carefully. Writing a strong directive thesis statement is foundational to writing a good argumentative paper. Remember, your thesis statement should be a simple declarative sentence but should also contain enough detail such that the thesis statement is definitive.

Research your topic in a way that does not waste time. Choose key words before you go to the library or search online. For instance, if you are writing your paper on the electric car replacing the gasoline dependent traditional car, some of your key words might be: energy saver, economics and car industry, air pollution, gas emissions, etc. This will cut down on your research time. Evaluate your sources and make sure any research you use is generally no more than five years old.

When writing your paper, remember to give your reader any background information needed to understand your argument. Do not assume your reader is as informed as you are on your topic. Once your paper is written, put it aside for a day or so before you proofread it. Print out your paper. Do not attempt to locate your errors while reading your paper on a computer screen. When revising your paper ask yourself the following:

- What is your main point? How might you clarify your main point? Do your other points follow one another logically?
- Who is your audience? Have you considered their needs and expectations? Your parent or professor is not your only audience.
- What is your purpose? Have you accomplished your purpose with this paper?
- Did you properly cite all your research sources?
- How effective is your evidence? How might your strengthen your evidence?
- Do you need to revise your thesis statement? Does every part of your paper relate back to your thesis? How might you improve these connections?
- Did you follow instructions and answer the appropriate questions?
- Did you adhere to the word count? Is your paper long enough ? Is it to long?
- Have you made any errors with grammar, punctuation, or spelling? How can you correct these errors?
- What might someone who disagrees with you say about your paper? Did you address these opposing arguments in your paper?

Finally, remember your paper should not merely inform. It should convince your reader of a significant point.

Write the Perfect Research Paper

Final Instruction for College Assignments

Writing assignments in college differ as much as instructors. There is no one guidebook, approach, or set of rules that college teachers will consult when putting together their coursework. Since each assignment will always be unique, it is important to devote time to thoroughly understanding what is being asked of you before beginning. Don't wait until the night before the work is due to begin asking questions and delving in. The sooner you understand and approach the assignment's requirements, the less time you will spend second-guessing (and needlessly revising) your writing.

Analyzing an Assignment

You will likely encounter many different kinds of writing assignments in college, and it would be nearly impossible to list all of them. However, regardless of genre, there are some basic strategies one can use to approach these assignments constructively.

Read the assignment sheet early and thoroughly.

An assignment sheet may be lengthy, but resist the temptation to skim it. Observe and interpret every detail of the text. Moreover, it is essential to focus on the key words of the subject matter being discussed.

It would be unfortunate to hand in an incomplete or misguided assignment because you did not properly read and understand the guidelines. Since you can easily overlook details on the first reading, read the assignment sheet a second time. As you are reading, highlight areas where you have questions, and also mark words you feel are particularly important.

Ask yourself why your professor has given this assignment. How does it relate to what you are studying in class? Pay attention to key words, such as *compare*, *contrast*, *analyze*, etc. Who is your audience? Should the paper be written in a formal or informal tone? Is there documentation required? If a specific number of sources are required, how many must be books vs. online sources? What type of citation is called for: APA, MLA,

Chicago, etc.? Is there a page or word count minimum/maximum? Are you required to submit a draft before the final copy? Will there be peer review?

Gets answers to your questions.

After thoroughly reading the assignment sheet, you might not have questions right away. However, after reading it again, either before or after you try to start the assignment, you might find that you have questions. Don't play a guessing game when it comes to tackling assignment criteria--ask the right person for help: the instructor. Discuss any and all questions with the person who assigned the work, either in person or via email. Visit him or her during office hours or stay after class.

Do not wait until the last minute, as doing so puts your grade at risk. Don't be shy about asking your professors questions. Not only will you better your understanding and the outcome of your paper, but professors tend to enjoy and benefit from learner inquiry, as questions help them rethink their assignments and improve the clarity of their expectations. You likely are not the only learner with a question, so be the one who is assertive and responsible enough to get answers.

In the worst case scenario, when you have done all of these things and a professor still fails to provide you with the clarity you are looking for, discuss your questions with fellow classmates.

Writing Centers.

Many colleges and universities have a writing center. Tutors are helpful consultants for reviewing writing assignments both before and after you begin. If you feel somewhat confident about what you need to include in your writing assignment, bring your completed outline and/or the first draft of your paper together with your assignment sheet. Tutors can also review your final draft before its submission to your professor.

Many writing centers allow you to make appointments online for convenience and may also have "walk-in" availability. It is a good idea to check out the available options a week or so in advance of when you will actually need the appointment, or even longer if it will be during mid-term or finals week.

Write the Perfect Research Paper

Create a timeline.

Set due dates for yourself, whether they be to have a topic picked or a whole rough draft completed. Procrastination rarely results in a good paper. Some school libraries offer helpful computer programs that can create an effective assignment timeline for you. This is a helpful option for new, inexperienced writers who have not yet learned the art of analyzing assignments, and who are not familiar with the amount of time that is required for the college writing process. Remember, late papers may or may not be accepted by your instructor, and even if they are your grade will likely be reduced. Don't sell yourself short with late submissions.

Prewriting and Brainstorming

Every writing assignment from every discipline requires the formulation of complex ideas. Thus, once the assignment guidelines have been thoroughly considered, you should begin to explore how you plan structure your work in order to meet them. While this is often considered to be the start of the writing process, it is also an essential part of assignment analysis, as it is here that the assignment is broken down into the most digestible parts. Such a process can be done either individually or in a group, depending on the situation.

Sample Assignments

As discussed earlier, instructors will come up with any number of assignments, most of which will stress different types of composition. In each section below, there are sample assignment directions and suggestions on how to proceed. What follows is not meant to be a comprehensive list of assignments, but rather a short list of the most common assignments you can expect to see in an introductory English course. Many assignments not listed here are simply creative variations of these basic directives. For example, you could approach a visual analysis the same way you would a rhetorical analysis; an argument paper is similar to a research paper, perhaps with a shorter argument. The techniques you use in writing a narrative can also translate into writing a short story or observational essay.

Cheryl R. Carter

Important Advice Before You Begin Writing

How do I pick a topic?

Have you ever been stressed out because you can't think of a good topic for an important writing assignment? You're not alone. As a learner, you'd probably prefer it if professors would just assign topics rather than leave you to find one on your own. However, professors aren't vague because they want to punish you; they usually just don't want to constrain your creativity or discourage you from writing about topics that truly interest you. Professors also want to be surprised by their learners' ingenuity, and very few teachers want to read a big stack of essays all on the same stale topic. Unfortunately, just being told to "be creative" is unlikely to calm you down when you've got a major paper due next week and still haven't found a topic to write about!

You should also look for an issue that you can reasonably cover given the time and space (page count) you have available. After that it's a simple matter of supporting your argument by bringing in relevant quotations from those who agree with you. You should also identify the counter-arguments and provide pertinent background information.

Ways to Get Ideas

Still stuck even after pouring over all those books and journals? Don't worry. There are plenty of other ways to stimulate your brain.

In general, though, remember that good ideas may arise anytime and anywhere. You might be struck by a brilliant insight as you're running on the treadmill or even while dreaming. Always be prepared to record new ideas. Carry a small notepad with you or use your mobile phone to record a voice memo. You might even try writing the idea on a napkin and taking a picture of it. The important thing is to get it down quickly, because you're all too likely to forget all about it by the time you're ready to write.

Another good way to generate ideas is to read and listen actively. Your texts and professors will discuss relevant issues in the field, and they might make comparisons to related ideas and other thinkers. A professor might say, "There is still work to be done in this area," or "there is great controversy over this issue." Be alert to these sources for good ideas. The biggest mistake a novice writer can make is to rely solely on "inspiration." As a scholar, you are never alone--don't be afraid to listen and respond to the work of others instead of always trying to be original or profound.

Even chatting with your classmates might help you think of a good topic. You can also check with your college or university's writing center. Many of them have tutors who can help you find and hone a great topic for your paper.

Let's look now at three other techniques for getting those brain juices flowing: brainstorming, clustering, and freewriting.

Brainstorming

Brainstorming allows you to quickly generate a large number of ideas. You can brainstorm with others or you can brainstorm by yourself, which sometimes turns into freewriting. To effectively brainstorm, write down whatever ideas come to mind. Sometimes it works better to write down each idea on a separate piece of paper. It also helps to ask yourself some questions:

1. What do I care about or what am I interested in?
2. What do I know that I could teach others?
3. What irritates me?

In order to capture more of your thoughts, you may want to brainstorm a few times until you have enough ideas to start writing.

Examples

Imagine you are in a class. Your instructor says you will have to write a paper on your favorite free-time activity, and that you must also persuade your reader to try it.

First ask yourself, *What do I care about?* or *What am I interested in?*

It is easiest to write about a topic that you are interested in. This could be anything from gardening to ice skating, or from writing poetry to playing the piano. Your list, in this example, would then read:

1. gardening
2. ice skating
3. writing poetry
4. playing the piano

At this stage, every idea is good since you are trying to come up with as many ideas as possible.

Second, ask yourself, *What do I know that I could teach others?*

You may be able to teach someone else something that you really enjoy. Good for you! If you cannot, don't worry; you are still just brainstorming. Perhaps you teach swimming lessons or t-ball, or maybe you bake really well and are able to offer some of your insights. Your list, in this example, would then read:

1. swimming lessons
2. t-ball
3. baking

Anything is fine. You are still brainstorming.

In academic writing with a less personal slant, the source of irritation is often another writer/theorist with whom you disagree. Your "irritation" then would lead to an effective piece about why you have a better conception of what's really going on. A less direct version of this would be a writer/theorist who makes some good points but lacks something in his/her argument that you can add to the "conversation."

A majority of academic writing begins with brainstorming. Go ahead! Try one or many of the ideas for brainstorming either by yourself or in a group. Working together to come up with ideas means that there are more ideas coming from many different minds.

A Graphic Organizer

Write the Perfect Research Paper

A graphic organizer (sometimes called clustering, webbing or mind mapping) is a process in which you take your main subject idea and draw a circle around it. You then draw lines out from the circle that connect topics that relate to the main subject in the circle. Clustering helps ensure that all aspects of the main topic are covered.

Example

After using the brainstorm example, let's say you decided on gardening as your topic. Your main idea of gardening would be in the center of your page circled. Anything else that you want to say about gardening you would connect to the circle with lines. You can also add more lines to extend the ideas that relate to thoughts around the circle. When finished, your clustering might look like the following:

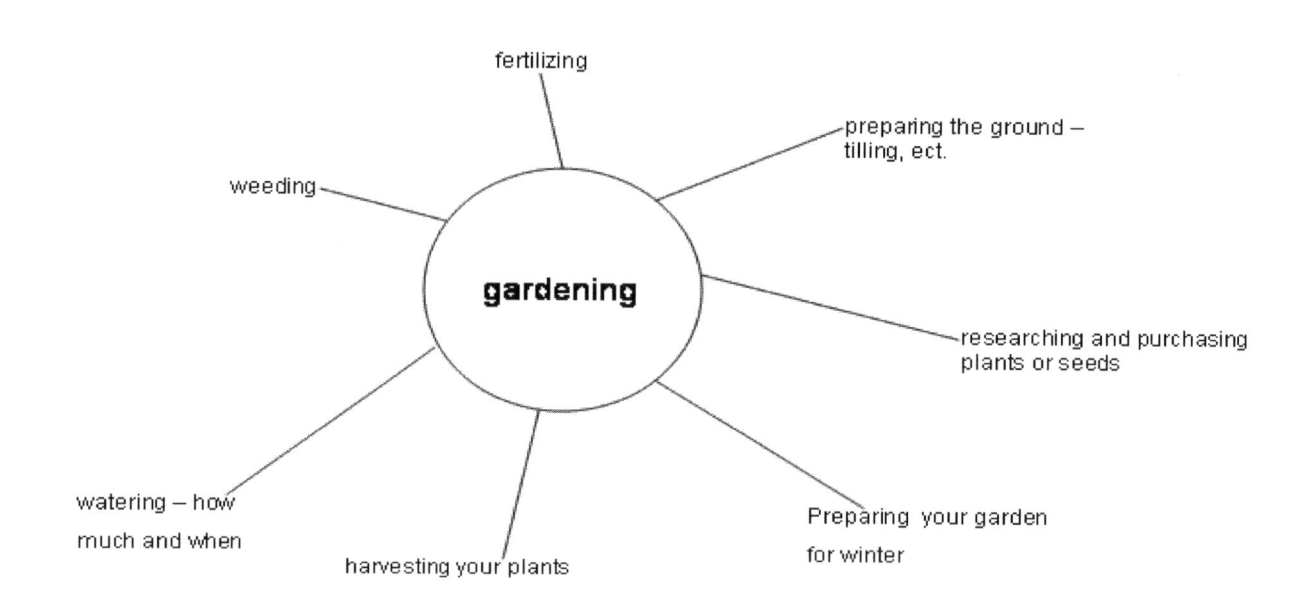

- fertilizing
- preparing the ground — tilling, ect.
- weeding
- **gardening**
- researching and purchasing plants or seeds
- watering – how much and when
- harvesting your plants
- Preparing your garden for winter

Cheryl R. Carter

What is Freewriting?

Freewriting helps generate ideas and set them in motion. To begin, start writing without worrying about spelling or grammatical errors. You should write your ideas naturally and spontaneously so that you can record many ideas quickly. Do not look back at what you wrote until you are satisfied that you have written enough. An easy way to freewrite is to set a time limit and then begin writing. You can write anything at all, and in the end, you will often find some quality ideas scattered throughout your writing.-

Example

1. I set my kitchen timer for a specific amount of time. Let's say 5 minutes.
2. I just begin writing without worrying about what I am putting onto the page.
3. The timer went off, so I stop writing.
4. At this point, I review what I have written and decide which point(s) to elaborate on.

With these simple writing tips, you should be able to find a topic and begin the process of writing the assigned paper. Established authors use brainstorming, clustering, and freewriting, so you're in good company when you use these techniques to help you overcome writer's block or writing anxiety. What works for someone else may not work for you. After all, these prewriting strategies are just ways to put your ideas on the paper so you can develop them at a later time. Try to enjoy the process of writing instead of seeing writing only as the chore of finishing an assignment your instructor has given you. Done this way, writing might become a pleasure that can also improve your critical thinking ability.

Write the Perfect Research Paper

How Do I Make an Outline?

Developing an outline, such as the examples below, can be helpful because you can keep an overview of what you want to say, check whether you have covered everything, and find what is out of scope and should be excluded. The outline can grow during the writing process as new points come to mind.

Outline example I

I. Introduction and Thesis

> Brief description of issues that arise when reading "Hamlet"

II. Issues of feminism uncovered through reading "Hamlet"

> a. What other scholars have discovered about feminism in "Hamlet"
> b. Which of these discoveries was most evident to me and how
> c. Ideas of feminism that I uncovered on my own

III. How uncovering ideas of feminism in "Hamlet" has led me to better understand what Shakespeare thought of the role women played in society IV. Conclusion

---

A sample outline.

Outline example II

I. Mixed marriages

> States this issue briefly, why I am interested in exploring this, and whether this issue exists in my culture

II. Issues of mixed marriage within your culture

> a. Is it acceptable to get married to a person who is a different religion?
> b. Is it acceptable to get married to a person who is a different race?
> c. What are the advantages or disadvantages of mixed marriages?

III. Personal experiences

      a. An example from my own life or my family.

      b. An example from the news.

IV. Conclusion

Advice on Writing Style

Keep your writing simple. Each sentence should contain one main idea. Sentences do not need to be long or complicated in order to do this.

Write complete sentences.

Avoid pretentious, silly language. Try not to use a long and difficult word when you can express the same idea more clearly with a short, easy word. Try not to use unusual, confusing metaphors.

Avoid biased, opinionative writing. Report objectively on events and let the facts speak for themselves.

Avoid the passive voice unless you have to use it.

Avoid obsequious, lengthy acknowledgments of advisors, teachers in charge of activities and so forth.

Avoid exaggerating or lying. Do not write simply for the sake of filling space. If there is very little to say about something, then say very little about it.

Avoid writing anything rude, offensive or vain.

Many of these ideas are taken from George Orwell's essay, Politics and the English Language - a must read for anyone interested in writing professionally. Read the essay here:

Here's an example of poor style:

A touch of lipsticks, a pat of powder on our so beautiful faces, eyebrows plucked, hairs all in place. A final look into the mirror: perfect faces for the evening. Dressing in lavish, shimmering gowns, as beautiful as angels on the tops of Christmas trees, the F. 5 girls sallied forth into the Conrad International Hotel for the celebration of their magnificent schooldays. There was an air of excitement filling the air in addition to the scrumptious aroma of the exquisite selection on the buffet counter. It was the much anticipated Graduation Dinner.

Far better would be:

The F. 5 Graduation Dinner took place on Friday, 26th June in the Harbour View Ballroom of the Conrad International Hotel, where graduating learners enjoyed a sumptuous buffet. The F. 5 girls wore formal evening gowns for the occasion, and also put a lot of effort into preparing their hair and make-up. Everyone looked splendid.

Another example:

The stamp-collecting club has as its aim and objective to promote interest in stamp-collecting. Although being the co-ordinator of stamp-collecting club has not been an easy task for me because of I had to organize many activities that related to stamp-collecting, but I learnt about leadership skills. This has been a very fruitful year for our club and all our members successfully collected stamps. I would like to thank my members for their eager stamp-collecting skills and my dearest vice-chairlady, secretary and PRO for their tireless efforts in trying to assist me in running this important activity. Also, we must express our sincere and heartfeltest gratitude to our teacher advisor, Mr. Terence Stamp. Without you our club would not have been so successful!!! We LOVE you, Mr. Stamp!

This would be far better:

This year has been very successful for the stamp-collecting club. We were able to attract more than 50 learners to join the club, and our increased membership has made it possible for us to organize a wider range of activities than in previous years. Learners particularly enjoyed the visit to the General Post Office in December and the talk on first-day covers by Mr. Wally Tang, the chairman of the Hong Kong Philately Society, in March. We are very grateful to Mr. Stamp for his help in organizing these activities

Write the Perfect Research Paper

College Reading Strategies

While you may be faced with more reading in college, you can easily adapt to the pace. Begin your reading your textbook or journal articles by looking at the pictures, charts or graphs. This will help you get a feel for what you are going to be reading about. Textbooks often have summaries so you may find it helpful to read the summary first before the chapter to get an overview of the material. Don't rush, take your time. Go through the details to comprehend the text as you read it. Read as much as you are able. When you start getting bored or need a break, take one. Reread the material. It is okay to reread something if you do not understand it fully the first time.

Use context clues to find out a word's meaning. Context clues help you figures out the meaning of a word by seeing how the word is used in a sentence. If you find a word that you're *totally* stumped on ,then us a dictionary. Reread if you don't understand what you are reading, in. Try reading the words out loud to yourself. If you still don't understand something, you might want to visit the college's tutoring lab or the campus' disability office. Do not panic if reading large portions of text is challenging for you. Many students struggle with understanding what they are reading. To actively read take notes while you are reading and remember to take frequent breaks so your eyes can rest. Finally, be actively engaged in the reading process. Do not read in bed. Instead, sit up and maintain the right posture.

The SQ3R and PQRST methods below are trusted methods you can use to maximize your reading in college

The SQ3 R Method

The SQ3R method is also a useful method and can be used with a wide range of material. As with most study skills, using the SQ3R method takes a bit of extra time, but in the end, it is worth it The SQ3R method can be used with a wide range of material, including English, History, Science, Math, and related subjects. As with most study skills, using the SQ3R method takes a bit of extra time, but in the end, you save time.

1. Survey

    The first step, survey or skim, advises that one should resist the temptation to read the book and instead glance through a chapter in order to identify headings, sub-headings and other outstanding features in the text. This is in order to identify ideas and formulate questions about the content of the chapter.

2. Question

    Formulate questions about the content of the reading. For example, convert headings and subheadings into questions, and then look for answers in the content of the text. Other more general questions may also be formulated:

    - *What is this chapter about?*
    - *What question is this chapter trying to answer?*
    - *How does this information help me?*

3. Read (R^1)

   Use the background work done with "S" and "Q" in order to begin reading actively. This means reading in order to answer the questions raised under "Q". Passive reading, in contrast, results in merely reading without engaging with the study material.

4. Recite (R^2)

   The second "R" refers to the part known as "Recite/wRite" or "Recall." Using key phrases, one is meant to identify major points and answers to questions from the "Q" step for each section. This may be done either in an oral or written format. It is important that an adherent to this method use his/her own words in order to evoke the active listening quality of this study method.

5. Review (R^3)

   The final "R" is "Review." In fact, before becoming acquainted with this method a student probably just uses the R & R method; Read and Review. Provided the student has followed all recommendations, the student should have a study sheet and should test himself or herself by attempting to recall the key phrases. This method instructs the diligent student to immediately review all sections pertaining to any keywords forgotten

Cheryl R. Carter

PQRST – Reading Strategy

Preview the Reading 1. Write the title of the section on your paper and underline it. 2. Write the subtitles of the different sections of the main title. 3. Write the bold words and their definitions from the section. 4. Look at the pictures and read their captions. Write your own title for each of the pictures. 5. Make a prediction about what the section is about and write it down. Example: "I think this reading will be about how cells work in our bodies." Question 6. Write a question you think the reading will answer.

Read 7. Write down the time you start reading and the time you finish the reading.

Summarize 8. Write down 3-5 sentences that explain what the reading was about.

Test 9. Test your question from #6. Do you know the answer now? If yes, write the answer. If no, write a new question that the reading did answer, then write the answer to that new question.

Preview

1. Title

2. Subtitles

3. Bold Words

4. Pictures

5. Prediction

Question

6. Question

Write the Perfect Research Paper

Read

7. Start Time

   End Time

Summary

8. 3-5 sentences

Test

9. Answer to Question #6

Summary/ Response Paper

Before writing a summary, it is important to use your critical +reading skills. First, read the article carefully. It might help to write down the main point of each paragraph in the margin next to it. Next, reread the article and look carefully for the main points the author is trying to get across. Look for things the author states explicitly, as well as what is implied by things that are not clearly stated. Look for any biases or missing information. Ask yourself questions while you read, such as "what is the big picture here? What is the author really trying to get across with this or that example?" The title will often provide a clue about the author's main point.

Most of all, slow down and take the time to reread the article several times. In summarizing an article, think about how you would explain its message to someone who hasn't read it. What are the main points of the piece? What is necessary to know about the work in order to understand it?

While writing a summary is a familiar assignment from grade school, in college, summaries are no longer enough, and instructors will frequently require a response. Writing a response is giving your opinion about the text. However, statements such as "I did/did not like it" are not sufficient. Not only must you be more descriptive with your opinions, but you need to support them. If you do not think that an author provided enough information to prove his or her point, state the specific flaws and what could be done to improve them. The same rule applies for any emotions felt while reading the text. Instead of just saying the writing made you sad, point out a specific passage in the text that made you feel that way. Talk about the word choices the author used and how that affected your reading.

Part Three

Research Excellence

"Tell me and I'll forget; show me and I may remember; involve me and I'll understand." .... 不闻不若闻之，闻之不若见之，见之不若知之，知之不若行之；学至于行之而止矣 [不聞不若聞之，聞之不若見之，見之不若知之，知之不若行之；學至於行之而止矣] Bù wén bù ruò wén zhī, wén zhī bù ruò jiàn zhī, jiàn zhī bù ruò zhīzhī, zhīzhī bù ruò xíng zhī; xué zhìyú xíng zhī ér zhǐ yǐ.

Cheryl R. Carter

Research Writing Basics

Studies indicate we learn more about a topic when we write about it and digest the information. We know that we understand a subject when we are able to teach it to others. A research paper presents your ideas and findings to others. Most English instructors will have you use Modern Language Association citations. *Write to Achieve* uses MLA for citations. Once you go to college, you may be required to use American Psychological Association (APA) or *Chicago Manual of Style* guidelines. Many Christian colleges use Chicago citations. Links to these are provided below.

The Modern Language Association is the standard for writing English papers. It provides consistency and credibility and protects you from plagiarism. Additionally, an instructor may want to reference information in your paper.

Research papers have a standard format. They are double-spaced throughout except for long quotes that are more than four lines. Your headings go on the front page, left corner. Even if homeschooled, you should get in the habit of submitting a paper formally in the correct MLA format. Pages are numbered in the upper right corner. You should use your last name and the page number, for example, "Carter 12."

Proper citation of your sources in MLA style can help you avoid plagiarism, which is a serious offense. There are two ways to cite in MLA, parenthetical citations (within the paper) and a "Works Cited" page (at the end of the paper). When you quote word for word within a paper, you must use quotation marks around the material and cite your source. You should also cite when you paraphrase or summarize a source. Widely accepted information does not need to be quoted. For instance, if you were writing about dairy farmers, you would not need to cite the fact that farmers rise early.

Quotes in essays are cited with the author's last name and page number(s) of the quote. For instance, *television viewing "dulls the minds and senses" (Smith, 547)* or *Smith stated that television viewing "dulls the mind and senses" (547)*. If the author's name is included in the text, just the page number is required. See the simplified MLA sheet for further information.

Citation helpers, particularly for college learners (and college-bound learners):

http://www.sourceaid.com/citationbuilder/

http://easybib.com/

http://www.calvin.edu/library/knightcite/index.php

http://www.zotero.org/

Cheryl R. Carter

Topical Paper

> **Purpose:** The purpose of a topical paper is to think analytically about a subject you have been studying. General subjects such as math, history or science make excellent topical papers.

Step One: Choose a topic

Choose a subject such as United States history; then, within the subject, choose a topic—for instance, western expansion. Think about everything you know (or have already learned) about the topic. The task of this assignment is to answer the question, what have I learned about this subject? Ask yourself what else you want to know, and include these findings in your final paper. Write those questions down and search for the answers.

Step Two: Determine what you know about the topic

Respond to the questions below. Think of your own questions. Look in the dictionary, encyclopedia, books, on the Internet, and at the library for sources that will help you answer the questions.

What have I learned about?

What made the individual, event, concept, or time period significant?

Why is this individual event, concept, or time period important? Why should I study it?

How is this individual event, concept, or time period important?

What vocabulary is important?

When is this individual event, concept, or time period relevant?

Where does this fit into my body of knowledge, or why am I studying this topic?

Write the Perfect Research Paper

Step Three: Order your question responses

Put the answers to your questions in order so they make sense. Number them. Use index cards so that you can change the order.

Step Four: Make an outline

Turn your numbered response questions into a simple outline. You should have approximately three paragraphs.

Outline

I. Introduction paragraph. List what you have learned. Use your strongest point as the hook.

II. Topic sentence (with the main point you want to make).

    First response

    Second response

    Third response

III. Topic sentence (with the final point you want to make and summary).

    First supporting point

    Second supporting point

    Third supporting point

    Concluding sentence

Step Five

Write your paper based on your outline.

Step Six: Proofread your paper

Proofread your paper for spelling, grammar, and structural issues. Use the rubric to determine the requirements of the paper are met.

Cheryl R. Carter

Research Précis

> **Purpose:** *A précis is a summary of a work that maintains the integrity of the work or the ideas of the original.. A précis is a brief accurate summary of a work. A précis is not a paraphrase because a paraphrase is often as long as the original work. A précis is significantly shorter. Generally, it is one-quarter to one- third the size of the original work. A précis gives the core of the message of a text and eliminates redundant words, lengthy*

Step One: Determine the main idea/theme of the text

Read the work or journal article carefully, attempting to grasp the main idea of the text. Look for the topic sentence or key repeating words or themes. This will help you understand the mind of the author. Topic sentences also offer clues as to the main ideas of a text or study.

A précis is not a miniature version of the text; it is a new work itself, so do not merely copy the text verbatim. You must maintain the viewpoint of the author, even if you disagree with it. A research précis should contain the thesis or purpose of the research and the methods used. It should also contain the results or the insight from the research, key words, and important data.

Step Two: Determine the most important parts of the research

Key answers to questions will help you determine the vital portions of a research précis.

What was studied (argued, discussed)?

How it was done (what was the focus)?

What was learned?

What does it means (why is it important)?

Write the Perfect Research Paper

Step Three: Write the précis

Write the précis based on the answers to the above questions. Use index cards with the responses on it, so you can determine the most important aspect of the research.

Step Four: Proofread

Proofread your paper for spelling, grammar, and structural issues. Use the rubric to ensure you met all the requirements of the assignment.

Cheryl R. Carter

Informational Research Paper

> **Purpose:** *The purpose of a high school research paper is to show the teacher that you can retrieve information you have studied and make it meaningful. Your paper should be thoroughly researched and should illustrate a comprehensive understanding of the topic you are studying. The typical high school paper uses a 12-point font with one-inch margins and is 5-10 pages long.*

Step One: Choose a topic

Generally, you will be asked to choose a topic that interests you, although it must be relevant to something you have studied in high school. Brainstorm by using a graphic organizer or jot down every possible paper-related idea that occurs to you. Eventually, you must narrow the focus of your idea. For instance, you cannot just write a paper on Native Americans. You need to write about some aspect of Native American life, ideals, trade, dress, habitation, etc.

The thesis statement must be somehow debatable. It cannot just be an informational statement, such as *Native Americans traded with others*. Most learners find it best to ask a question and pose an answer that is a bit controversial. For instance, if you are studying American history, you might ask why some of the settlers and some of the native people had conflicts.

You would then pose a controversial response, such as: *The settlers and native people had conflict because neither trusted the other.* You could then build an argument based on the fact that you believe distrust drove the relationship in an unpleasant direction. Of course, another learner could easily disagree and cite instances of the native people working peacefully alongside the settlers. This makes the thesis statement debatable and a perfect way to begin a paper.

Opposing views of an argument should be mentioned, even if you do not delve fully into those opposing views. By showing both sides of the conflict, you prove to your teacher that you have done significant research and made an informed decision.

Write the Perfect Research Paper

Step Two: Write your thesis

Once you have narrowed your topic and assured yourself that the subject is debatable, compose a thesis statement. The thesis statement has to be strong, because it will drive the entire paper. In this instance, your thesis statement is: *Settlers and native people had conflict starting when the first European foot hit the American shore because neither trusted the other.* To construct an effective thesis statement, state your opinion, make a point, take a stand, have a slant, provide perspective, and set out to prove something. Begin boldly with a challenging or provocative assertion; you can always refine your approach later. Your thesis has to be strong, because it will guide the entire process.

Step Three: Research your topic

Turn your thesis statement into a question and research the topic by attempting to answer the question. For the above thesis statement, you might ask, why did the settlers and native people distrust one another? You might also ask, how do I know they distrusted one another? What evidence can I find to prove my thesis statement is correct?

Use index cards to jot down information you gather on these questions. When writing the information on the cards, sort the research into sections. For instance, if you were writing a paper on American wars, you would write each war on top of an index card before you take the notes. Make sure your notes are clear. Remember to write down the name of the book, article, chapter, etc. Do not rely on your memory; record the information on the source right away on the index cards.

You should write a summary or paraphrase your notes while you are gathering research material. Use quotes in your paper, but do not use an excess of quotes, because it will make your paper seem a bit stiff. You should research extensively. It is better to have too much rather than too little research.

Step Four: Organize your research

After you have completed all of your research, use a graphic organizer to brainstorm how you would likely organize your research. Turn the graphic organizer information into a linear outline. Write the outline noting a possible topic sentence for each paragraph. Your paper should have an introduction and at least three points to expound on once you start writing the paragraphs. Your conclusion will probably be one paragraph. Depending on the type of report you are writing, your conclusion will answer the question, so what? Remind your readers why the information in your paper is important. Your conclusion might challenge your readers to take action based on the information in your paper or show your readers how your topic fits into a larger issue.

The length of your paper will determine your outline. You should basically outline each paragraph.

II.   Introduction paragraph.

This includes your thesis and provides a brief background of what you will be writing on in your paper.

II. Topic sentence (with the main point you want to make)

    First supporting point

    Second supporting point

    Third supporting point

II. Topic sentence (with the point you want to make)

    First supporting point

    Second supporting point

    Third supporting point

III. Topic sentence (with the point you want to make)

    First supporting point

    Second supporting point

    Third supporting point

IV. Topic sentence (with the point you want to make)

    First supporting point

    Second supporting point

    Third supporting point

V. Conclusion

Step Five: Write the paper based on the outline

Write your paper based on your outline. This should be very easy, especially if you have written the outline based on the length of the paper. Longer papers require longer outlines, and shorter pages require a more concise outline. Remember to include transitional terms at the end or beginning of paragraphs so that papers flow logically.

Step Six: Proofread

    Proofread your paper for spelling, grammar, and structural issues. Use the rubric as your guideline.

Cheryl R. Carter

College Research Paper

> **Purpose:** *A college research paper is different from a high school research paper. It is more comprehensive in scope.*

The keys to a well-written college research paper are:

1. You must make a strong argument. The argument should not be obvious. It should be provocative or controversial.
2. It must be informative as well as analytical. There must be a balance of both of these qualities throughout the paper.
3. The paper should force the reader (who is not just your professor) to form an opinion after reading your paper; therefore, your arguments must be very convincing.
4. The paper must literally be an intellectual conversation between you (the writer) and your readers.
5. You must build on your argument and keep the paper on track. It is essential that your paper have a strong beginning, middle, and end.

There are definite steps that are essential to forming an A+ research paper. The steps are not necessarily sequential. All writing is a bit recursive.

Step One: Choose a topic

Generally, your professor will allow you to choose the direction your paper may take. In English class, you will definitely have more liberty to choose a topic of your liking. You should choose a topic that interests you and one that you know enough about to present a strong argument. Your instructor may give you a broad subject, such as population control. You will then have to do a bit of preliminary research to narrow the paper to a finite subject that you can handle. Perhaps you might examine population control in Haiti after the earthquake. Note the topic is specific, targeted, and narrow enough to provide focus for the paper. Once you begin doing the research you will be able to ascertain if a topic is too narrow.

Write the Perfect Research Paper

The purpose of the paper will help you determine how to choose an appropriate topic. You must know the paper's purpose before you write your thesis statement. Purpose is determined by what the professor wants. Professors generally want to see you applying logic and thinking critically about your research. Take time to brainstorm your ideas. Push yourself to think critically about your research.

Step Two: Thesis statement

Write your thesis statement. Your thesis statement is the essential building block for your essay. The thesis serves a twofold purpose: 1) It is the foundation of your paper; it will guide you in research and assist you in forming your paper; and (2) it helps the reader to follow your argument.

Do not underestimate the importance of the thesis statement, because a poorly developed thesis statement will lead to a poorly written paper. If the topic is assigned by your professor, you can easily form a thesis statement by asking a question based on the topic. For instance, if you have to write on nuclear reactors, you could ask the question *Should nuclear reactors be placed in heavily populated areas?* or you could ask, *Does the cost of nuclear reactors justify their existence given the current budget crisis?* Your question is not a thesis statement, but it can get you to start thinking about your thesis statement. If the subject of the paper is assigned, it is important that you choose a topic that separates you from other learners, because the topic will be known to your professor.

A thesis statement should be clear and direct. Your position should be asserted right away. The reader should know the conclusion of your argument and what you want to consider, believe, or be persuaded to do. In short, you should express your main idea, give the conclusion of the matter, and tell the reader why he/she should agree with you. This should be done in one or two sentences. The strongest thesis statement is stated in just one sentence, although it is reasonable to write two sentences when writing comprehensive papers.

A strong thesis takes a position; this position is often confrontational, controversial, or questionable, and it is specific. It also opens the door for discussion on the issue. For instance, this is not a good thesis statement:

> *There are negative aspects to population control.*

It is too vague. What does the writer mean by *negative aspects*? It can easily be rectified by stating precisely the negative aspects to population control. Over the years, I have found that when learners use terms like *good*, *bad*, *negative*, or *successful* in their thesis statements, their thesis statements tend to be poorly written. These thesis statements do not necessarily have to be discarded; I merely ask learners to revise their thesis statements by asking them to replace vague adjectives with more specific statements. For instance, the above thesis statement might be revised: *Studies show large families contribute to the stability of the society, and thus population control should be discouraged.*

Here, the author defined one of her negative aspects. An even stronger thesis statement might be: *Population control is immoral and should not be determined by the government, because the government has proven itself ineffective in making decisions that benefit the family. In fact, historically the family has suffered for generations as the result of governmental population control.*

Note that this thesis statement is two sentences long. Do not confuse the length of this thesis statement with its effectiveness. A thesis statement can be strongly stated in one sentence. In fact, many professors prefer a one-sentence thesis statement.

A thesis must have all elements operating together to form an actual thesis statement. You cannot just state a fact or observation and expect it to be a thesis. For instance, the following is not a thesis statement:

The United Nations growth charts indicate population control efforts have increased twofold over the past ten years.

Write the Perfect Research Paper

This is a specific statement of fact. It does not propose an argument. Argument is an essential element when composing a thesis statement.

Your professor may not ask you what your thesis statement is. He/she may assume that you know what a thesis statement is because it is an essential ingredient in college writing. Your thesis statement always appears in your first paragraph. Review what a thesis statement is in this curriculum.

Remember, a thesis statement is the foundation and road map to your entire paper. It:

1. Makes a claim that invites discussion and/or dispute;
2. Tells the reader what you want him/her to believe or be persuaded to do; and
3. Is specific and stated clearly.

Step Three: Research

Research should be done in phases. The first phase is to research your topic and to probe your thesis statement. This is what I call the soft research stage. The soft research stage is like putting your toe in the frigid, rolling waters at the seashore to test the temperature of the water. If the temperature is too cold (i.e., you are unable to find anything on your topic), your topic may be too narrow. Conversely, if you find too much material on your topic, your thesis statement may be too broad. After this soft research stage, you may need to change your thesis statement. Ideally, you should research a topic before you compose a final thesis statement and be guided by the purpose of the paper, which is what your professor wants to see in the paper.

The purpose of your paper should drive your research. Purpose determines your approach; you will know how to approach the paper based on the requirements of the paper. Specifically, take notice of the words your instructor uses. If he/she asks you to analyze the problem, he/she wants you to look at your topic in pieces and then form conclusions about the whole. For instance, he/she may want you to look at how and/or why population controls are established, or the smaller elements that define population growth, before addressing the broader issues. If you are asked to describe a problem, the instructor wants to see your thoughtful reflections or interpretation in your own words. You should always research with the paper's purpose in mind.

Once you have established your thesis statement and know your paper's purpose, you should proceed to the second stage, which I call "serious research." In high school, you were allowed to write papers using materials from popular magazines, general Web sites, and even daily newspapers. These kinds of sources are unacceptable in college research papers. You must gather your information from scholarly sources.

Scholarly research sources have distinct characteristics. The author usually has an advanced degree. The material is generally peer reviewed. Popular sources, on the other hand, are written for the public; they tend to be short and have no academic reference. A scholarly article usually includes an abstract, or article summary, and generally has graphs, charts, footnotes, endnotes, and a bibliography. *Ulrich's Periodical Directory* maintains a listing of scholarly publications. University presses and other noted publishers produce scholarly books. Once you have determined your sources are correct, you are ready to delve into the research process.

Some reliable online scholarly research Web sites include: H*ighbeam.com*, J*stor.org*, S*cholar.google.com*, and D*oaj.org*. Once you are in college, you will have access to the college's library.

Step Four: Take notes

As you read or skim through each source, take copious notes. Think about the direction you would like your paper to take. Make cursory notes by jotting down some key ideas from your research. Write the main idea on top of the paper and use a different page for each idea. For instance, suppose you had two points you wanted to make about population control; they might be government regulation and opposition. You would then title each page with your idea and record the notes under each subject. See the note card example at the end of the research section. These cursory notes will assist you in making notes that are more comprehensive.

The bulk of your time should be spent collecting and organizing the information for your research paper. You will need index cards. I recommend three-by-five cards but you can use five-by-eight cards if you need more room. Document your source on the back of the index card. This includes author, periodical volume, date, etc. On the front of the card, place your notes. Write legibly. See the sample of the card at the end of the research paper section.

Accurate note taking will help you avoid plagiarism. Plagiarism is not just repeating a source verbatim; it is also taking someone's ideas and claiming them as your own. Instructors disapprove of plagiarism and consider the theft of intellectual ideas just as weighty as the crime of robbery. You may want to keep your note cards even after you have written your paper to verify your research.

There are four basic kinds of research notes. The most obvious kind of research note is the quotation note. Quotation notes are the exact expressions of a source and are generally enclosed in quotation marks. An example might be: *Gertrude Dugger believes, "All nations will engage in some kind of population control by the end of this century."*

Notice that it is verbatim, exactly what the author has said. At times, a quote is used in conjunction with your own words. For instance: *Population growth is not important "unless you consider the termination of an entire generation as nonexistent fact."*

Paraphrasing is when you take the essence of what the author has said and put it in your own words. You must cite the reference when you paraphrase, and you should change the sentence structure a bit. For instance, suppose the sentence is: *The bored boy walked to the store to get the candy.* You cannot say: *The unmotivated lad strolled to the grocery to get the candy.*

The sentence structure is the same and basically every word is the same. This is unacceptable. You can say: *The candy did not entice the boy; he still walked to the grocery store.* Note that you will have to know the author's intent in order to paraphrase successfully.

Summary notes are a strong mainstay of many research papers and differ from paraphrased notes in that they do not provide a point-by-point note transfer; you simply need to capture the essence of the information or the key thoughts. Often when you read a great deal of information, especially redundant data, you can easily summarize the information. Your instructor will not ask you whether you used a paraphrase or summary note but you should nonetheless know the difference so you can vary the kinds of notes you use in your paper.

Précis is another kind of note. A précis note differs from a summary note in that it may be longer. It generally summarizes a complete article. When writing a précis note, you should read the passage carefully. Pay attention to the author's tone, intent, and viewpoint, and take note of key phrases. Think of a précis as an abridged note.

Field notes include research your teacher may ask you to conduct, interviews, questionnaires, experiments, tests, or measurements. These kinds of notes will need to be developed into charts, graphs, or laboratory notes.

Finally, you should document your personal notes. As you read through the material, you will begin to form your own opinions. Capture your thoughts right away by writing them down. You also do not want your thoughts to mingle unconsciously with the material you are collecting. It is also a good idea to take time and write down your thoughts once you have completed all of your research.

Step Five: Make an outline

Your outline will serve as your paper's road map. It shows the order in which information will be presented or the argument will be made. An outline will help you keep the information logical. An outline breaks down your thesis in a clear and logical matter. It is imperative that the reader is able to follow the argument. At this point, you should ask yourself if your points do indeed prove your thesis. Your subpoints should support or explain your main points. It is essential that you weed out any poor or ineffective points or arguments while you are forming your outline. You may use your cursory notes, which were broken down topically as a guide. You can organize your note index cards into an outline once you identify your main points. Your subpoints would then follow your main points. The basic format for an outline uses an alternating series of numbers and letters, indented accordingly, to indicate levels of importance.

Parallelism is also important when creating an outline. If you use full sentences for one point, you should use sentences for all of your points. Your outline should include your introduction and conclusion. Give thought to how you will begin as well as end your paper. Your outline may be tweaked as you examine your notes or research a bit more.

Write the Perfect Research Paper

You can also add notes to the outline. This actually makes writing your paper even easier because you have the topic sentences and the information. When you make your outline, do not throw away any extra research that you may have done, because you may need it later, especially if your paper does not meet the minimum page requirement.

Introduction

- Define the problem.
- Give background information.
- Set up facts for your thesis.
- State the thesis.

Supporting paragraph—analyze the issue based on your first major point.

- Discuss and examine the issue.
- Find a transition to your next point.

Discuss your findings.

- Restate your thesis.
  - Interpret the findings.
  - Provide answers, solutions, or a final opinion.

Step Six: Write your draft

After you have written your outline interspersed with notes, it is time to begin the writing process. If you have spent sufficient time developing the outline, this step should be fairly easy, because the outline will help you to present your argument logically and with sufficient details. Your opening sentence has to be striking, such as an astounding statistic, fact, or questionable statement. It should be a bit startling to the reader. After you make the statement, provide some background information to frame your argument, and then state your thesis without apology.

Unlike a high school paper, your college reading audience determines your approach. The paper should be written as if you are addressing a specific group. For instance, suppose you are writing about a conservative issue and your readers are liberals. You would have to find common ground and build your argument slowly and methodically. If you are writing to a general audience, assume they have no background knowledge and slowly build your case.

If you are writing to an amicable audience, jump right into your arguments and do not waste time discussing common ground. Many learners assume their teacher is the sole audience; this is not the case in college writing. You should write as if addressing a group. Once you know your audience, you can then build your argument.

Your thesis statement is your claim; you then provide reasons to support your claim. Of course, these reasons have been derived from your notes. The three basic persuasive techniques are:

(1) Ethos, which is essentially credibility due to position or authority. Cite noted authorities throughout your paper.

(2) Logos, which is presenting information in a logical and sequential matter with facts that back up your points. Your outline with notes will help you present your case line by line and precept by precept such that your points are strong. When readers follow the validity of an argument, they are more likely to accept your argument.

(3) Finally, pathos appeals to the emotions of the reader and his/her goals, values, and beliefs.

Other ways to persuade your reader include repetition. As you present your points, reiterate your thesis statement throughout and continue to provide reasons why the reader should embrace your point of view. This involves having strong reasons that logically back up your argument. It is essential that you first get the reader to accept a part of your argument and then invite him/her to take an intellectual step further.

Write the Perfect Research Paper

Your reader needs to understand your argument completely; use metaphors, similes, and analogies so that connections can be made. Use empathy or show that you can understand the position of those involved in the issue. Predict the future based on your argument. People want to know what will happen in the future. You may flatter the reader by suggesting that responsible, mature, and open-minded people embrace your ideas. Be careful not to be obvious. Address objections. This is a vital part of your paper. You should have already written the opposing view. Use anecdotal stories. People inherently enjoy stories. Stories are a strong yet subtle form of persuasion.

Compose your paper based on your outline with these techniques in mind. Each individual paragraph should be focused on a single idea that supports your thesis. Begin paragraphs with topic sentences, support assertions with evidence, and expound your ideas in the clearest, most sensible way you can. Your conclusion should reinforce your opening paragraph as well as the body of the paper. You do not need to repeat the points verbatim, but you should find a way to summarize your points. If you find your paper is too short, you can go back and add examples or add a bit more of the opposing views. If you need to cut anything, you can summarize some of your points a bit more. Add your citations and reference list (see the example).

Step Seven: Revise your paper

Review the syllabus and make sure your paper adheres to your teacher's guidelines. Go over the following checklist. Now is the time for documentation. There is no reason to memorize citations because they are readily available on the Web.

MLA—Used by English, literature

APA—Psychology

Chicago

Allow for time before your paper's completion, so you can find your mistakes.

Cheryl R. Carter

Graphic Organizers

One step at a time (Crawl before you walk)... 循序渐进 [循序漸進] Xún xù jiàn jìn

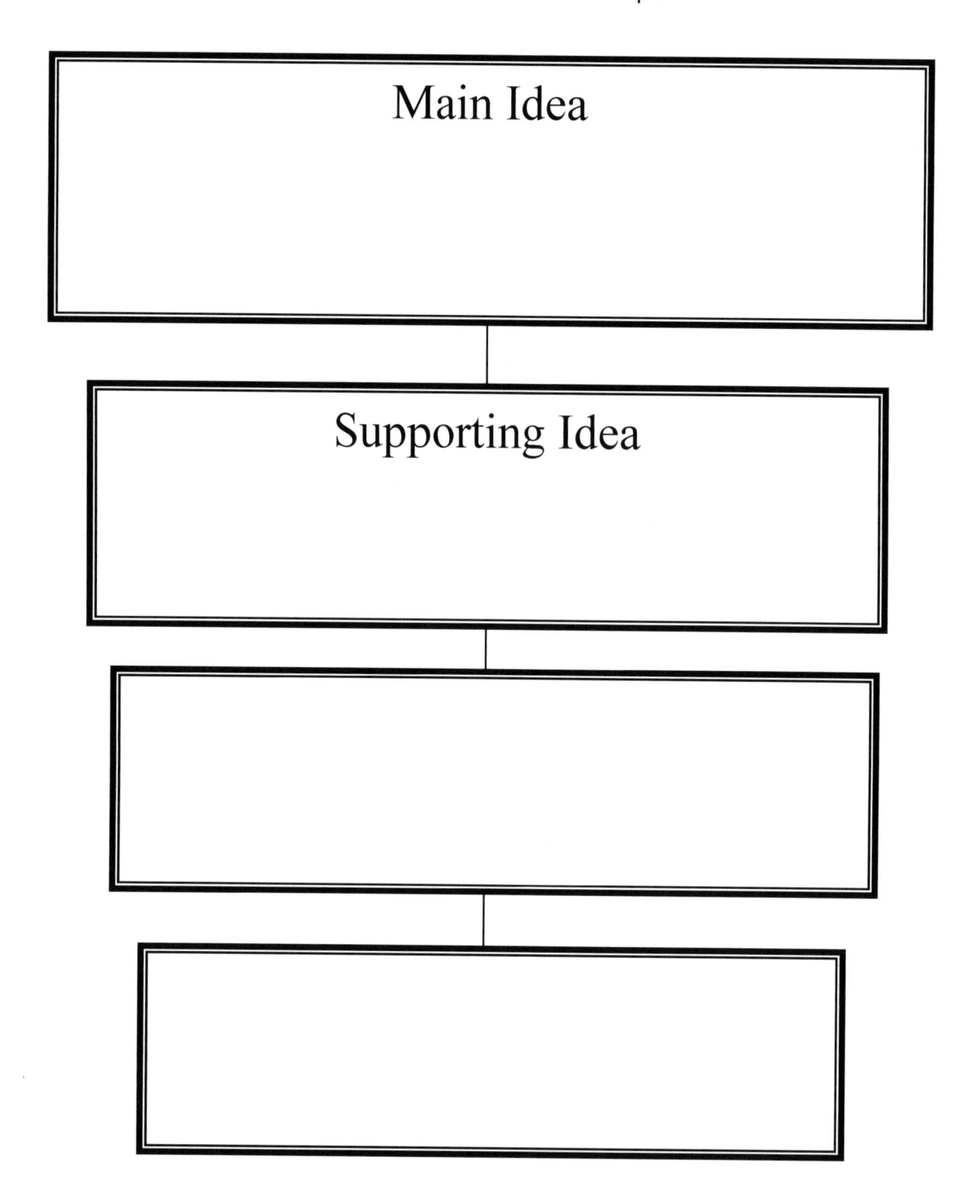

Write the Perfect Research Paper

Main Idea

Supporting Idea

Main Idea or Thought

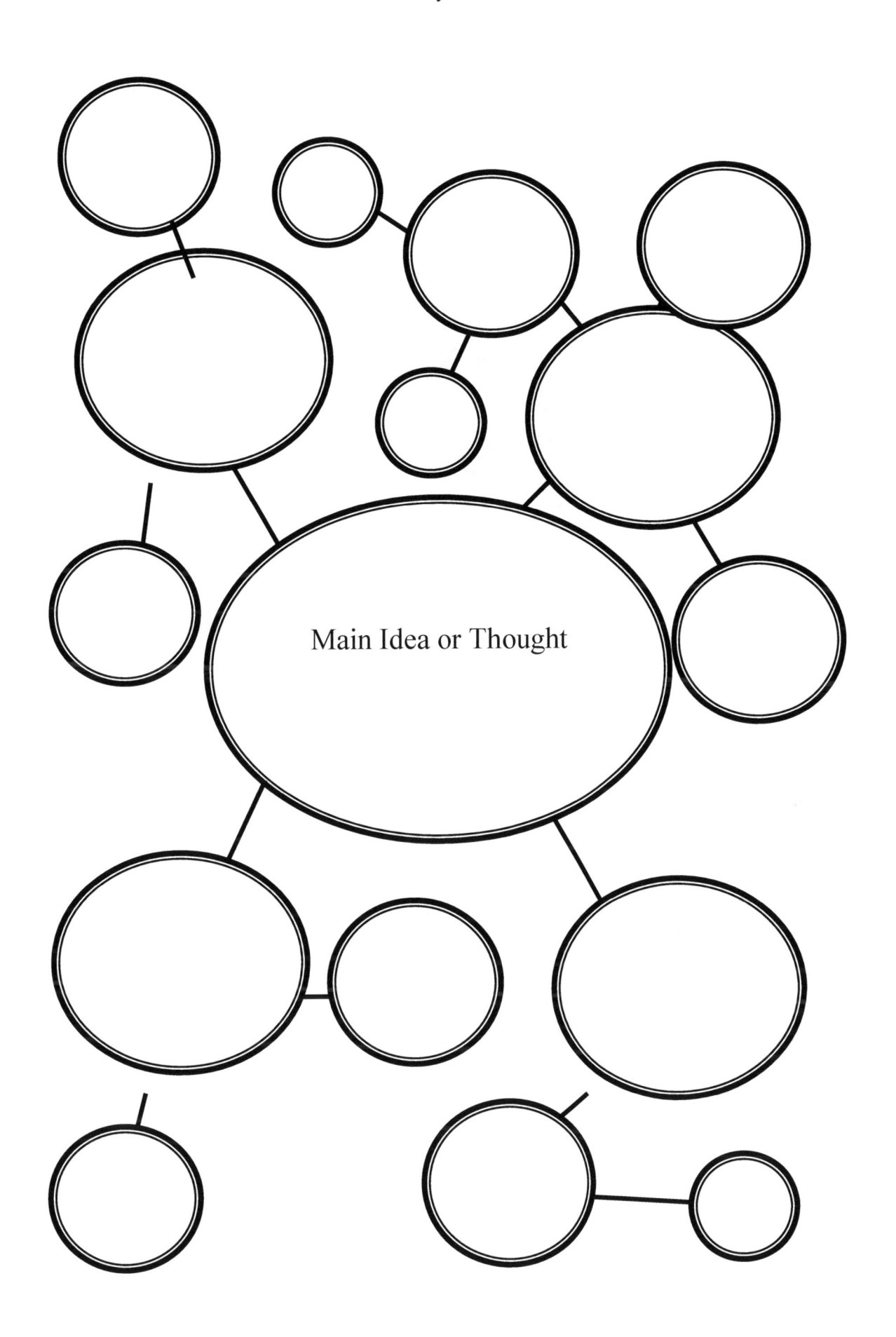

Sample Research Papers

Learning is a treasure that will follow its owner everywhere... 学习是永远跟随主人的宝物 [學習是永遠跟隨主人的寶物] Xuéxí shì yǒngyuǎn gēnsuí zhǔrén de bǎowù]

Cheryl R. Carter

Informative Essay

  Every writer experiences that moment: she walks into a bookstore, looks at the nearest display of whatever book is the "hot seller" that week, and wonders, "How can someone write something *that bad* and get published, but I can't?" The publishing industry is known for being hyper-competitive and almost as fickle as the field of fashion design. With thousands of talented, unknown writers vying to get discovered, sometimes it seems like the answer to the question of "who gets a publishing deal this week" is as random, and as risky, as a game of Russian roulette. Writers seeking to take control of their careers and their lives need to re-evaluate the typical publishing cycle and consider whether or not self-publishing is a viable option. Self-publishing is an accessible means of pursuing the business of authorship, allows a writer to exercise more control over her intellectual property, and gives a writer the flexibility to promote her writing in a way that she finds acceptable and effective.

  The opportunities to self-publish a novel, novella, short story, article, or any other preferred format of writing have never been more prevalent. Self-publishing platforms such as Amazon, Lulu, and Smashwords offer abundant options in a variety of mediums, from physical trade paperbacks to the ever-growing eBook sector. Writers can select from a wide variety of packages, including editing and proofreading services, cover design options, and formatting services. Multi-talented writers can even take on all of these lofty tasks themselves and just pay a nominal fee for offering their works through the plethora of online distributors. With big online retailers such as Amazon investing significant resources into offering self-publishing tools for budding authors, writers with a finished manuscript can find plenty of opportunities to create and stage their final products.

  Naysayers claim that those who self-publish should beware releasing a book that hasn't received the blessing of big publishing houses because once something is published, it can never be un-published. The collective response from those familiar with intellectual property rights has been a resounding, "So what?" Writers who self-publish have a distinct advantage over those who sign contracts: self-publishers retain the intellectual property rights for their work, which means they can keep their work, or sell it whenever they want. Traditionally published authors simply can't; the publishing house gets all of the rights, while the author only remains entitled to future royalties, however stingy. Having control over a copyright can be a powerful bargaining chip, giving self-published authors who prove themselves their choice of publishers if they later decide to go the traditional route.

Publishing houses have the resources necessary to launch an effective marketing campaign for a newly published author. However, many authors lament the lack of backing they get from their publishers once their book goes to print, or may even disagree with a particular public relations angle for moral or strategic reasons. When self-publishing, the writer is the one who maintains control. The writer selects the venues, content, and target demographic, and decides what strategies will be most effective for reaching the readers she wants to reach. From blog entries to Twitter feeds, print ads, submissions, and book reviewers, writers can find new readers just about anywhere with a little time and some social media savvy.

The accessibility of self-publishing tools, advantages in intellectual property rights, and opportunities for unique self-directed promotional campaigns all make self-publishing a more viable option for writers looking to share their work without having to wait for a big publishing contract. Any writer who is tired of rejected query letters, returned manuscripts, and unfavorable publishing contracts should explore this rapidly growing venue. Writers are uniquely positioned to take control of their professional lives and their industry by developing a supportive readership before getting drawn into a less-than-desirable book deal. Self-publishing is truly the way of the future for any writer with a little time, a little talent, and a lot of ambition.

Cheryl R. Carter

A New Constitution and a History of "Democracy"

A glance at the late 18th century U.S. political system reveals that the new Constitution was the law of a highly undemocratic land. The early United States was a society in which entire sections of the population were denied basic human rights, where the institutions of the new government were not derived from egalitarian principles, and where millions of people did not receive adequate political representation. As the overarching political instrument of the era, the Constitution bears responsibility for a society in which the many toiled without representation for the benefit of a powerful few.

Perhaps the most egregious example of the Constitution's anti-democratic features was its sanction of the widespread practice of slavery. Rather than ending slavery, the Constitution allowed planters and others to hold their fellow human beings as chattel. Not only did the Constitution permit the existing system of slavery to continue, it permitted the Atlantic slave trade to keep "importing" slaves for 20 more years. It counted a slave as three-fifths of a human being; moreover, this provision was inserted not to protect the rights of the enslaved but to boost the electoral power of the slave states. Such a provision was not the only institutional failure of the Constitution.

The arrangement of the new federal government in the Constitution was highly unrepresentative. The president was elected indirectly through the Electoral College, while the Supreme Court was completely appointed. In the remaining branch of government, the upper house, the Senate, provided for each state to have equal representation without regard for how many people lived in the state. By diluting the power of the franchise, the Constitution made a system that was destined to be unrepresentative even more undemocratic. Only the House of Representatives nominally derived its power from the people, and its character was deeply affected by who could and could not vote.

The Constitution allowed states to set norms for who could vote in elections and who could not. In the early United States, that meant that people who did not own sufficient property, enslaved people, and women were denied the vote. A government allegedly founded on the idea of "no taxation without representation" violated this rallying cry of the American Revolution. As a result of the Constitution, a majority of people in the early United States could not vote for their representatives.

Rather than promoting a government "of the people, by the people, and for the people," the Constitution sanctioned practices and structured institutions that were unrepresentative. Ordinary people, whether because they were enslaved, because they were women, or because they were working-class people, lived and worked without any real power. Instead, a small minority of wealthy and powerful men ruled over the majority of the population; the source of their power was the undemocratic Constitution of the United States.

Cheryl R. Carter

Research Papers

    Just as animals around the world have evolved to better survive in their environments, botanical life everywhere has also been forced to grow and adapt to their habitats. Every plant—from the smallest strain of seaweed to the tallest redwood—is the result of billions of years of competition for optimal growth conditions. In many places with harsh conditions or where there is a very large population of plants competing for limited resources, some plants have developed amazing ways of surviving. Some are poisonous to prevent animals from killing and eating them, while others have become carnivorous, eating and digesting insects to make up for a lack of nitrogen that most plants would absorb through soil. The greatest example of plant adaptation, however, is found in a unique succulent, more commonly known as the cactus.

    The majority of cacti are made up of four simple parts: the stem, the needles, the flowers, and, like all plants, the root system. The stem of a cactus acts as the plant's water storage system. Once water is drawn in through the roots, it can be stored in the stem for long periods of time, allowing the cactus to live through the long periods of drought and intense heat for which deserts are so well known. While most plants absorb sunlight and photosynthesize through their leaves throughout the day, for most succulents, these vital processes are also performed by the bulky stem. All plants have stomata, or pores, on them that allow them to breathe in carbon dioxide necessary for photosynthesis. When these pores open to let in the gas, water vapor escapes. This is fine for most plants, but in a desert habitat, this precious water evaporates rapidly. To prevent this, cacti open their stomata at night, when it is significantly colder and much less likely to evaporate. "Their problem then is that, as the carbon dioxide cannot be turned into sugar in the dark, it has to be stored in the form of organic acids. The cell sap of the succulent thus becomes more and more acidic as its night-storage acid batteries become fully charged" (Bellamy). When the sun rises, the plant once again closes its pores and begins taking in sunlight, which allows it to complete the process of photosynthesis by turning the stored acids into glucose, or sugar. This unique succulent trait is called crassulacean acid metabolism and is something most people would not expect from a mostly branchless plant covered in spikes.

Write the Perfect Research Paper

Despite having few other plants providing competition, succulents have had to overcome some of the harshest living conditions on the planet. Extremely high temperatures during the day and evening temperatures that often dip below freezing are only the beginning of problems for desert plant life. Scarce rainfall coupled with very dry air make it difficult for plants to obtain water needed for photosynthesis and create competition between animals and plants. Desert-dwelling animals also have problems obtaining water, but unlike plants, which are rooted in one place and are very limited in the ways of defense, animals are free to eat whatever plant life they can to acquire water or simply move to an area where it is easier to obtain water and nutrients. The competition provided by desert animals attempting to acquire water from plants has led to the cactus's most obvious and distinctive evolution: its hard, sharp spines or needles.

Needles are arguably the most important part of all cacti and are without a doubt the most obvious sign that a plant is in fact a succulent. The reason needles are so vital to cactus survival is because they protect the plant's stem, where photosynthesis is performed and water is stored. Without this protection, cacti would still be suited for desert living because of their unique methods of surviving the extreme temperatures, but they would also be an incredibly popular source of food and water for desert animals. While some animals have evolved to work around these hard, sharp protectors and crack into the juicy innards of the plant, these spines have been keeping cacti alive for thousands of years: "Spines have been known to persist unchanged on the trunk of giant Suaharos several centuries old" (Hylander). It is a widely known fact that the most well-armored cacti grow in the hottest areas. In these areas, the heavy lattice of needles can help to block some of the sun's rays, keeping the cactus from overheating and the water inside from evaporating even with the stem's tightly closed pores.

While the needles of succulents often make the plants look hazardous, inhospitable, and sometimes just plain ugly, when they flower in the spring, they are some of the most beautiful plants on the planet. Many cacti flower only at night, closing up during the day because the flowers themselves are often very sensitive to the relentlessly bright rays of the sun. Some of these beauties are so delicate that they only bloom for a single day—or even mere hours in some cases. The flowers come in a variety of different shapes, sizes, and colors, although the night-blooming flora is often mostly white, making them easy to see in the dark:

> Some of the blossoms are six inches in diameter and twice that in length; many are broadly cup-shaped, others funnel-shaped; most have numerous sepals grading in color into the brilliantly scarlet, purple, yellow, or snowy white petals. Inside, is a golden tangle of stamens—three thousand of them in the Suaharo flower (Hylander).

Americans and Mexicans should be especially proud of this stunningly gorgeous plant, since the southwestern United States and Mexico are where the succulent family originated before it quickly spread as far north as Alberta and all the way south to the Straits of Magellan. All cacti found outside the American continents—even in Australia where they seem a natural part of the environment—were at some point introduced to the land from the Central American region. The only known exception to this is "some species of the Mistletoe Cactus, which are now native to South Africa, Madagascar, and Ceylon, brought as seeds to those countries from Mexico and South America by ocean flying birds" (Hylander). Many of the succulents that now grow in Asia were chosen specifically for their radiance.

There are many different species within the succulent family that are the specimens of ethnobotanical research because of their long history of use among the peoples native to the Central American region. Many of the cacti in the Trichocereus genus, such as the Trichocereus Pachanoi, the Trichocereus Peruvianus, and the Trichocereus Terscheckii, more commonly known as the San Pedro Cactus, Peruvian Torch Cactus, and Cardon Grande Cactus respectively, have been ingested in ritual ceremonies for thousands of years in the Americas for a chemical they produce called mescaline. Mescaline is a psychedelic which is also found strongly in the Lophophora Williamsii, or Peyote Cactus. It is described by Richard Evans Schultes as causing:

> a period of contentment and over-sensitivity, and a period of nervous calm and muscular sluggishness, often accompanied by hypocerebrality, colored visual hallucinations, and abnormal synesthesiae. Alterations in tactile sensation, very slight muscular incoordination, disturbances in space and time perception, and auditory hallucinations may accompany (Schultes).

Write the Perfect Research Paper

Other cacti, such as the Agave Tequilana Azul or Blue Agave, are grown and cultivated specifically for distilling with alcohol for a unique taste. The Blue Agave plant has been used for around five centuries, and is still the preferred choice today, as the plant from which tequila is distilled.

The succulent family is, without a doubt, one of the plant world's most evolved species. Their many unique traits make them perfect for survival in the cruel, inhospitable desert environment. Needless to say, most other plants would not be able to live with the high daytime temperatures, low nighttime temperatures, intense sunlight, and anything goes attitude of the desert's natural animal life. Not only are cacti the prime example of the plant world's ability to overcome all odds, but they are also the pride of both North and South America, having enjoyed a long and rich heritage in the New World. Cacti have recently begun to sink their roots into the other continents, both literally and figuratively. Many species are valued in Europe and Asia for their fierce beauty, while others seem completely natural on the continent of Australia. Succulents are a proud family of plant that will continue to grow, flourish, and be respected by humans wherever they find themselves on Earth for millennia to come.

Works Cited

Bellamy, D. 1983. Bellamy's new world. London, England: The British Broadcasting Company. 192 p.

Cotton, C. 1996. Ethnobotany: principles and applications. West Sussex, England: John Wiley and Sons Ltd. 424 p.

Erowid. 2007. Psychoactive Cacti Vault. http://www.erowid.org/plants/cacti/cacti.shtml. May 10, 2008.

Hylander, C. 1947. The world of plant life. New York, New York: The MacMillan Company. 722 p.

Shultes, Richard Evan. The Appeal of Peyote (Lophophora Williamsii) as a Medicine American Anthropologist New Series, Vol. 40, No. 4, Part 1 (Oct. - Dec., 1938), pp. 698-715. Blackwell Publishing on behalf of the American Anthropological Association. http://www.jstor.org/stable/661621. May 10, 2008.

Schultes, R, von Reis S. 1995. Ethnobotany: evolution of a discipline. Portland, Oregon: Dioscorides Press. 441 p.

Write the Perfect Research Paper

The introduction of foreign species to Hawaii has greatly affected the populations of the islands' native species. In many cases, the introduction of foreign species has wiped out the entire population of certain species, rendering them extinct. This is especially devastating because many of these species are endemic, meaning they are found only in one particular location and nowhere else in the world. The majority of species living in Hawaii are the result of thousands of years of island biodiversity. A few birds of one species migrate from some distant island due to some rare occurrence of nature and eventually evolve into several new species, each perfectly adapted to the environment in which it has come to live. Unfortunately, each of these endemic species is especially susceptible to the effects of invasive species, which means the impact on Hawaii's animal life has been tremendous.

When goats were first introduced to Hawaii by Captain Cook in the late 1700s, they immediately began eating all the local plant life. Most of these plants were unused to being preyed upon until the introduction of foreign species into their habitat, and so suffered massive population loss from grazing animals. The goat population, on the other hand, grew rapidly, as it had no natural predators to keep it in check. The introduction of European pigs to Hawaii had similar effects on the native species, although, due to a scarcity of protein in natural Hawaiian forests, the European pig population did not grow as rapidly as the goats until the 1900s with the introduction of earthworms and foreign plants which made up large portions of the pigs' diets (Stone and Loope 1987).

European pigs and goats are both primarily grazing animals, meaning their diet consists mostly of plant life found near the ground. Rats, mice, and mongooses, however, are easily able to reach low hanging branches of trees containing fruit, seeds, and sometimes even bird nests. Mongooses were first introduced to Maui in the 1880s to prey upon rats in sugarcane fields and quickly extended their range to include almost every hospitable nook in the island. They feed on most plants and animals smaller than them, including lizards, insects, crabs, rodents, small birds, and especially eggs (Stone and Loope 1987). This large prey base of exotic species has allowed the mongoose population to increase in density and range, as well as enabling it to rapidly gain stability while expanding into new areas (Vitousek et al. 1987). Mongooses spread rapidly across the island of Maui, occupying space and devastating the populations of any native species in their territory. There has been much debate over whether or not the mongooses are a limiting factor on the native bird species of Hawaii, particularly the ground-nesting species, since they will often eat eggs and even gosling birds (Stone and Loope 1987).

Humans are not only indirectly responsible for the reduction and extinction of native Hawaiian species through the introduction of invasive species, but are also sometimes the direct cause. The Townsend's shearwater, one of the handful of surviving Hawaiian seabirds, are greatly affected by the light pollution from both urban and resort locations in Hawaii. These birds, whose breeding colonies were undiscovered until the late 1960s, are blinded and disoriented while flying from inland nesting areas to the coast, causing them to crash, often in the developed areas producing the lights, where they are usually killed by cars or household pets (Scott et al. 1988). Younger shearwaters are the most susceptible to being disoriented by light pollution; therefore, the majority of birds killed this way are too young to have reproduced, leading to a shearwater population of mostly older birds with few young to take their place and ensure the continued survival of their own species. This problem, first observed in 1961, has elevated as more and more land was developed in response to Hawaii's booming tourism in the 1970s. Recently, new methods have been put into action hoping to reduce including the use of light-blocking shields to reduce light pollution.

Works Cited

Scott, J.M., C.B. Kepler, C. van Riper III, and S.I. Fefer. 1988. Conservation of Hawaii's vanishing avifauna. BioScience 38(4):238-253.

Stone, C.P., and L.L. Loope. 1987. Reducing negative effects of introduced animals on native biotas in Hawaii: What is being done, what needs doing, and the role of national parks. Environmental Conservation 14:245-258.

Vitousek, P.M., L.L. Loope, and C.P Stone. 1987. Introduced species in Hawaii: Biological effects and opportunities for ecological research. Trends in Ecology and Evolution 2(7):224-227.

Write the Perfect Research Paper

Book Report

Proof of Heaven by Dr. Eben Alexander

As a neurosurgeon, Dr. Eben Alexander believed that there was no tangible proof of heaven or a spiritual afterlife. Though many of his own patients claimed they had spiritual experiences, Dr. Eben listened to their stories but always had rational explanations for everything they had seen and felt. Near-death experiences were nothing more than the innermost parts of the brain working overtime in a traumatic event to help ease the pain and fear of a patient. The mind can conjure up all kinds of visual pictures and ideas while being unconscious. Not until he had his own near death experience did he understand what his patients were talking about. In his book, *Proof of Heaven*, Dr. Eben Alexander explains his spiritual journey

A healthy, vibrant family man, Dr. Alexander was always more concerned about others than he was about himself—which is why, the morning he woke up with an excruciating headache, he ignored it so as to not worry his family. When he tried to get in the shower, pain shot through his back and head, and he had no choice but to go back to bed. Still, he told his worried wife to go about her business. He would take a small nap and wake up feeling fine. After some time passed and he had not awakened, his wife went to check on him. What she found was a lifeless, unconscious shell of her husband.

In a panic, she called emergency services, and Dr. Alexander was rushed to the hospital. After several tests, medicines, and scans, he was still not doing well and was actually falling deeper and deeper into a coma. He had less than 10% of his brain function left, and everyone was finally addressing the fear that they were going to lose him. While lying there unresponsive and barely alive on that bed, Dr. Alexander was experiencing something completely different.

As he explains it, he found himself in a brown, scary place where he had no idea who he was or where he was. It was not a place anyone would like to stay very long. After some time there (he did not have a sense of time so could not say how long), he saw a light and traveled to it. He went through different layers of the spiritual world until finally coming to the most peaceful, loving place he had ever been. Colors were beautiful and vibrant, and he was greeted by a beautiful guardian who picked him up on a butterfly wing as she showed him where he was. Communicating only telepathically, he could not only hear, but he could also feel the warmth, love, and compassion that surrounded him. He had no idea who he was, and he did not care. He had no memories and no thoughts of anything but the encompassing love. He never wanted to leave.

But somehow, he was falling back through the layers—falling away from that glorious place, and he had no idea why. He suddenly saw people who looked familiar, and as he approached his body, he started to feel the familiar human feelings. He realized that this was his family and that he had to come back because they were not ready to lose him yet. He returned to his body and miraculously had a full recovery.

Dr. Alexander allowed this event to transform his entire life, his work, and his beliefs. He no longer excluded others' near death experiences and instead compared them to his own. No longer a skeptic, he tried to convince his scientific colleagues of what he went though. They, in turn, humored him by listening but dismissed what he was saying. This has not deterred Dr. Alexander from trying to get his story out there, which is why he wrote *Proof of Heaven*. He is hoping that people will read, believe, and listen to what he went through, and he hopes that it causes his readers to make the same transformations in their own lives.

Bonus Classic Book that all Writers Should Have

Elements of Style

The classic Elements of Style contains sage advice that should be regularly reviewed by all college-bound learners:

II. Elementary Rules of Usage

1. Form the possessive singular of nouns with 's.

Follow this rule whatever the final consonant. Thus write,

Charles's friend

Burns's poems

the witch's malice

This is the usage of the United States Government Printing Office and of the Oxford University Press.

Exceptions are the possessives of ancient proper names in *-es* and *-is*, the possessive *Jesus'*, and such forms as *for conscience' sake, for righteousness' sake*. But such forms as *Achilles' heel, Moses' laws, Isis' temple* are commonly replaced by

the heel of Achilles

the laws of Moses

the temple of Isis

The pronominal possessives *hers, its, theirs, yours,* and *oneself* have no apostrophe.

2. In a series of three or more terms with a single conjunction, use a comma after each term except the last.

Thus write,

red, white, and blue
honest, energetic, but headstrong

He opened the letter, read it, and made a note of its contents.

This is also the usage of the Government Printing Office and of the Oxford University Press.

In the names of business firms the last comma is omitted, as

Brown, Shipley and Company

The abbreviation *etc.*, even if only a single term comes before it, is always preceded by a comma.

3. Enclose parenthetic expressions between commas.

The best way to see a country, unless you are pressed for time, is to travel on foot. This rule is difficult to apply; it is frequently hard to decide whether a single word, such as *however,* or a brief phrase, is or is not parenthetic. If the interruption to the flow of the sentence is but slight, the writer may safely omit the commas. But whether the interruption be slight or considerable, he must never omit one comma and leave the other. Such punctuation as

Marjorie's husband, Colonel Nelson paid us a visit yesterday,
or

My brother you will be pleased to hear, is now in perfect health,
is indefensible.

Non-restrictive relative clauses are, in accordance with this rule, set off by commas.

The audience, which had at first been indifferent, became more and more interested.

Similar clauses introduced by *where* and *when* are similarly punctuated.

In 1769, when Napoleon was born, Corsica had but recently been acquired by France. Nether Stowey, where Coleridge wrote *The Rime of the Ancient Mariner,* is a few miles from Bridgewater.

In these sentences the clauses introduced by *which, when,* and *where* are non-restrictive; they do not limit the application of the words on which they depend, but add, parenthetically, statements supplementing those in the principal clauses. Each sentence is a combination of two statements which might have been made independently.

The audience was at first indifferent. Later it became more and more interested. Napoleon was born in 1769. At that time Corsica had but recently been acquired by France.

Coleridge wrote *The Rime of the Ancient Mariner* at Nether Stowey. Nether Stowey is only a few miles from Bridgewater.

Restrictive relative clauses are not set off by commas.

The candidate who best meets these requirements will obtain the place.
In this sentence the relative clause restricts the application of the word *candidate* to a single person. Unlike those above, the sentence cannot be split into two independent statements.

The abbreviations *etc.* and *jr.* are always preceded by a comma, and except at the end of a sentence, followed by one.

Similar in principle to the enclosing of parenthetic expressions between commas is the setting off by commas of phrases or dependent clauses preceding or following the main clause of a sentence. The sentences quoted in this section and under Rules 4, 5, 6, 7, 16, and 18 should afford sufficient guidance.

If a parenthetic expression is preceded by a conjunction, place the first comma before the conjunction, not after it.

He saw us coming, and unaware that we had learned of his treachery, greeted us with a smile.

4. Place a comma before *and* or *but* introducing an independent clause.

The early records of the city have disappeared, and the story of its first years can no longer be reconstructed.
The situation is perilous, but there is still one chance of escape.

Sentences of this type, isolated from their context, may seem to be in need of rewriting. As they make complete sense when the comma is reached, the second clause has the appearance of an after-thought. Further, *and,* is the least specific of connectives. Used between independent clauses, it indicates only that a relation exists between them without defining that relation. In the example above, the relation is that of cause and result. The two sentences might be rewritten:

As the early records of the city have disappeared, the story of its first years can no longer be reconstructed.
Although the situation is perilous, there is still one chance of escape.

Or the subordinate clauses might be replaced by phrases:

Owing to the disappearance of the early records of the city, the story of its first years can no longer be reconstructed.
In this perilous situation, there is still one chance of escape.

But a writer may err by making his sentences too uniformly compact and periodic, and an occasional loose sentence prevents the style from becoming too formal and gives the reader a certain relief. Consequently, loose sentences of the type first quoted are common in easy, unstudied writing. But a writer should be careful not to construct too many of his sentences after this pattern (see Rule <u>14</u>).

Two-part sentences of which the second member is introduced by *as* (in the sense of *because*), *for, or, nor,* and *while* (in the sense of *and at the same time*) likewise require a comma before the conjunction.

If a dependent clause, or an introductory phrase requiring to be set off by a comma, precedes the second independent clause, no comma is needed after the conjunction.

The situation is perilous, but if we are prepared to act promptly, there is still one chance of escape.
For two-part sentences connected by an adverb, see the next section.

5. Do not join independent clauses by a comma.

If two or more clauses, grammatically complete and not joined by a conjunction, are to form a single compound sentence, the proper mark of punctuation is a semicolon.

Stevenson's romances are entertaining; they are full of exciting adventures.
It is nearly half past five; we cannot reach town before dark.

It is of course equally correct to write the above as two sentences each, replacing the semicolons by periods.

Stevenson's romances are entertaining. They are full of exciting adventures.
It is nearly half past five. We cannot reach town before dark.

If a conjunction is inserted, the proper mark is a comma (Rule 4).

Stevenson's romances are entertaining, for they are full of exciting adventures.
It is nearly half past five, and we cannot reach town before dark.

Note that if the second clause is preceded by an adverb, such as *accordingly, besides, so, then, therefore,* or *thus,* and not by a conjunction, the semicolon is still required.

I had never been in the place before; so I had difficulty in finding my way about.
In general, however, it is best, in writing, to avoid using *so* in this manner; there is danger that the writer who uses it at all may use it too often. A simple correction, usually serviceable, is to omit the word *so,* and begin the first clause with *as:*

As I had never been in the place before, I had difficulty in finding my way about.
If the clauses are very short, and are alike in form, a comma is usually permissible:

Man proposes, God disposes.
The gate swung apart, the bridge fell, the portcullis was drawn up.

6. Do not break sentences in two.

In other words, do not use periods for commas.

I met them on a Cunard liner several years ago. Coming home from Liverpool to New York.
He was an interesting talker. A man who had traveled all over the world, and lived in half a dozen countries.

In both these examples, the first period should be replaced by a comma, and the following word begun with a small letter.

It is permissible to make an emphatic word or expression serve the purpose of a sentence and to punctuate it accordingly:

Again and again he called out. No reply.
The writer must, however, be certain that the emphasis is warranted, and that he will not be suspected of a mere blunder in punctuation.

Rules 3, 4, 5, and 6 cover the most important principles in the punctuation of ordinary sentences; they should be so thoroughly mastered that their application becomes second nature.

7. A participial phrase at the beginning of a sentence must refer to the grammatical subject.

Walking slowly down the road, he saw a woman accompanied by two children.
The word *walking* refers to the subject of the sentence, not to the woman. If the writer wishes to make it refer to the woman, he must recast the sentence:

He saw a woman, accompanied by two children, walking slowly down the road.
Participial phrases preceded by a conjunction or by a preposition, nouns in apposition, adjectives, and adjective phrases come under the same rule if they begin the sentence.

Write the Perfect Research Paper

On arriving in Chicago, his friends met him at the station.	When he arrived (or, On his arrival) in Chicago, his friends met him at the station.
A soldier of proved valor, they entrusted him with the defence of the city.	A soldier of proved valor, he was entrusted with the defence of the city.
Young and inexperienced, the task seemed easy to me.	Young and inexperienced, I thought the task easy.
Without a friend to counsel him, the temptation proved irresistible.	Without a friend to counsel him, he found the temptation irresistible.

Sentences violating this rule are often ludicrous.

Being in a dilapidated condition, I was able to buy the house very cheap.

8. Divide words at line-ends, in accordance with their formation and pronunciation.

If there is room at the end of a line for one or more syllables of a word, but not for the whole word, divide the word, unless this involves cutting off only a single letter, or cutting off only two letters of a long word. No hard and fast rule for all words can be laid down. The principles most frequently applicable are:

a. Divide the word according to its formation:
know-ledge (not knowl-edge); Shake-speare (not Shakes-peare); de-scribe (not des-cribe); atmo-sphere (not atmos-phere);
b. Divide "on the vowel:"

edi-ble (not ed-ible); propo-sition; ordi-nary; espe-cial; reli-gious; oppo-nents; regu-lar; classi-fi-ca-tion (three divisions possible); deco-rative; presi-dent;
c. Divide between double letters, unless they come at the end of the simple form of the word:

Apen-nines; Cincin-nati; refer-ring; but tell-ing.
The treatment of consonants in combination is best shown from examples:

for-tune; pic-ture; presump-tuous; illus-tration; sub-stan-tial (either division); indus-try; instruc-tion; sug-ges-tion; incen-diary.

The learner will do well to examine the syllable-division in a number of pages of any carefully printed book.

III. Elementary Principles of Composition

9. Make the paragraph the unit of composition: one paragraph to each topic.

If the subject on which you are writing is of slight extent, or if you intend to treat it very briefly, there may be no need of subdividing it into topics. Thus a brief description, a brief summary of a literary work, a brief account of a single incident, a narrative merely outlining an action, the setting forth of a single idea, any one of these is best written in a single paragraph. After the paragraph has been written, it should be examined to see whether subdivision will not improve it.

Ordinarily, however, a subject requires subdivision into topics, each of which should be made the subject of a paragraph. The object of treating each topic in a paragraph by itself is, of course, to aid the reader. The beginning of each paragraph is a signal to him that a new step in the development of the subject has been reached.

The extent of subdivision will vary with the length of the composition. For example, a short notice of a book or poem might consist of a single paragraph. One slightly longer might consist of two paragraphs:

A. Account of the work.

B. Critical discussion.

A report on a poem, written for a class in literature, might consist of seven paragraphs:

A. Facts of composition and publication.

B. Kind of poem; metrical form.

C. Subject.

D. Treatment of subject.

E. For what chiefly remarkable.

F. Wherein characteristic of the writer.

G. Relationship to other works.

The contents of paragraphs C and D would vary with the poem. Usually, paragraph C would indicate the actual or imagined circumstances of the poem (the situation), if these call for explanation, and would then state the subject and outline its development. If the poem is a narrative in the third person throughout, paragraph C need contain no more than a concise summary of the action. Paragraph D would indicate the leading ideas and show how they are made prominent, or would indicate what points in the narrative are chiefly emphasized.

A novel might be discussed under the heads:

A. Setting.

B. Plot.

C. Characters.

D. Purpose.

A historical event might be discussed under the heads:

A. What led up to the event.

B. Account of the event.

C. What the event led up to.

In treating either of these last two subjects, the writer would probably find it necessary to subdivide one or more of the topics here given.

As a rule, single sentences should not be written or printed as paragraphs. An exception may be made of sentences of transition, indicating the relation between the parts of an exposition or argument.

In dialogue, each speech, even if only a single word, is a paragraph by itself; that is, a new paragraph begins with each change of speaker. The application of this rule, when dialogue and narrative are combined, is best learned from examples in well-printed works of fiction.

10. As a rule, begin each paragraph with a topic sentence; end it in conformity with the beginning.

Again, the object is to aid the reader. The practice here recommended enables him to discover the purpose of each paragraph as he begins to read it, and to retain the purpose in mind as he ends it. For this reason, the most generally useful kind of paragraph, particularly in exposition and argument, is that in which

the topic sentence comes at or near the beginning;

the succeeding sentences explain or establish or develop the statement made in the topic sentence; and

the final sentence either emphasizes the thought of the topic sentence or states some important consequence.

Ending with a digression, or with an unimportant detail, is particularly to be avoided.

If the paragraph forms part of a larger composition, its relation to what precedes, or its function as a part of the whole, may need to be expressed. This can sometimes be done by a mere word or phrase (*again; therefore; for the same reason*) in the topic sentence. Sometimes, however, it is expedient to precede the topic sentence by one or more sentences of introduction or transition. If more than one such sentence is required, it is generally better to set apart the transitional sentences as a separate paragraph.

According to the writer's purpose, he may, as indicated above, relate the body of the paragraph to the topic sentence in one or more of several different ways. He may make the meaning of the topic sentence clearer by restating it in other forms, by defining its terms, by denying the converse, by giving illustrations or specific instances; he may establish it by proofs; or he may develop it by showing its implications and consequences. In a long paragraph, he may carry out several of these processes.

1 Now, to be properly enjoyed, a walking tour should be gone upon alone.	1 Topic sentence.
2 If you go in a company, or even in pairs, it is no longer a walking tour in anything but name; it is something else and more in the nature of a picnic.	2 The meaning made clearer by denial of the contrary.
3 A walking tour should be gone upon alone, because freedom is of the essence; because you should be able to stop and go on, and follow this way or that, as the freak takes you; and because you must have your own pace, and neither trot alongside a champion walker, nor mince in time with a girl.	3 The topic sentence repeated, in abridged form, and supported by three reasons; the meaning of the third ("you must have your own pace") made clearer by denying the converse.
4 And you must be open to all impressions and let your thoughts take colour from what you see.	4 A fourth reason, stated in two forms.
5 You should be as a pipe for any wind to play upon.	5 The same reason, stated in still another form.
6 "I cannot see the wit," says Hazlitt, "of walking and talking at the same time.	6-7 The same reason as stated by Hazlitt.
7 When I am in the country, I wish to vegetate like the country," which is the gist of all that can be said upon the matter.	
8 There should be no cackle of voices at your elbow, to jar on the meditative silence of the morning.	8 Repetition, in paraphrase, of the quotation from Hazlitt.

9 And so long as a man is reasoning he cannot surrender himself to that fine intoxication that comes of much motion in the open air, that begins in a sort of dazzle and sluggishness of the brain, and ends in a peace that passes comprehension.—Stevenson, *Walking Tours.*

9 Final statement of the fourth reason, in language amplified and heightened to form a strong conclusion.

1 It was chiefly in the eighteenth century that a very different conception of history grew up.

1 Topic sentence.

2 Historians then came to believe that their task was not so much to paint a picture as to solve a problem; to explain or illustrate the successive phases of national growth, prosperity, and adversity.

2 The meaning of the topic sentence made clearer; the new conception of history defined.

3 The history of morals, of industry, of intellect, and of art; the changes that take place in manners or beliefs; the dominant ideas that prevailed in successive periods; the rise, fall, and modification of political constitutions; in a word, all the conditions of national well-being became the subjects of their works.

3 The definition expanded.

4 They sought rather to write a history of peoples than a history of kings.

4 The definition explained by contrast.

5 They looked especially in history for the chain of causes and effects.	*5* The definition supplemented: another element in the new conception of history.
6 They undertook to study in the past the physiology of nations, and hoped by applying the experimental method on a large scale to deduce some lessons of real value about the conditions on which the welfare of society mainly depend.— Lecky, *The Political Value of History*.	*6* Conclusion: an important consequence of the new conception of history.

In narration and description the paragraph sometimes begins with a concise, comprehensive statement serving to hold together the details that follow.

The breeze served us admirably.
The campaign opened with a series of reverses.

The next ten or twelve pages were filled with a curious set of entries.

But this device, if too often used, would become a mannerism. More commonly the opening sentence simply indicates by its subject with what the paragraph is to be principally concerned.

At length I thought I might return towards the stockade.
He picked up the heavy lamp from the table and began to explore.

Another flight of steps, and they emerged on the roof.

The brief paragraphs of animated narrative, however, are often without even this semblance of a topic sentence. The break between them serves the purpose of a rhetorical pause, throwing into prominence some detail of the action.

11. Use the active voice.

The active voice is usually more direct and vigorous than the passive:

I shall always remember my first visit to Boston.
This is much better than

My first visit to Boston will always be remembered by me.
The latter sentence is less direct, less bold, and less concise. If the writer tries to make it more concise by omitting "by me,"

My first visit to Boston will always be remembered,
it becomes indefinite: is it the writer, or some person undisclosed, or the world at large, that will always remember this visit?

This rule does not, of course, mean that the writer should entirely discard the passive voice, which is frequently convenient and sometimes necessary.

The dramatists of the Restoration are little esteemed to-day.

Modern readers have little esteem for the dramatists of the Restoration.

The first would be the right form in a paragraph on the dramatists of the Restoration; the second, in a paragraph on the tastes of modern readers. The need of making a particular word the subject of the sentence will often, as in these examples, determine which voice is to be used.

The habitual use of the active voice, however, makes for forcible writing. This is true not only in narrative principally concerned with action, but in writing of any kind. Many a tame sentence of description or exposition can be made lively and emphatic by substituting a transitive in the active voice for some such perfunctory expression as *there is,* or *could be heard.*

There were a great number of dead leaves lying on the ground.	Dead leaves covered the ground.
The sound of the falls could still be heard.	The sound of the falls still reached our ears.

The reason that he left college was that his health became impaired.	Failing health compelled him to leave college.
It was not long before he was very sorry that he had said what he had.	He soon repented his words.

As a rule, avoid making one passive depend directly upon another.

Gold was not allowed to be exported.	It was forbidden to export gold (The export of gold was prohibited).
He has been proved to have been seen entering the building.	It has been proved that he was seen to enter the building.

In both the examples above, before correction, the word properly related to the second passive is made the subject of the first.

A common fault is to use as the subject of a passive construction a noun which expresses the entire action, leaving to the verb no function beyond that of completing the sentence.

A survey of this region was made in 1900.	This region was surveyed in 1900.
Mobilization of the army was rapidly carried out.	The army was rapidly mobilized.
Confirmation of these reports cannot be obtained.	These reports cannot be confirmed.

Compare the sentence, "The export of gold was prohibited," in which the predicate "was prohibited" expresses something not implied in "export."

12. Put statements in positive form.

Make definite assertions. Avoid tame, colorless, hesitating, non-committal language. Use the word *not* as a means of denial or in antithesis, never as a means of evasion.

He was not very often on time.	He usually came late.

He did not think that studying Latin was much use.	He thought the study of Latin useless.
The Taming of the Shrew is rather weak in spots. Shakespeare does not portray Katharine as a very admirable character, nor does Bianca remain long in memory as an important character in Shakespeare's works.	The women in *The Taming of the Shrew* are unattractive. Katharine is disagreeable, Bianca insignificant.

The last example, before correction, is indefinite as well as negative. The corrected version, consequently, is simply a guess at the writer's intention.

All three examples show the weakness inherent in the word *not*. Consciously or unconsciously, the reader is dissatisfied with being told only what is not; he wishes to be told what is. Hence, as a rule, it is better to express a negative in positive form.

not honest	dishonest
not important	trifling
did not remember	forgot
did not pay any attention to	ignored
did not have much confidence in	distrusted

The antithesis of negative and positive is strong:

Not charity, but simple justice.
Not that I loved Caesar less, but Rome the more.

Negative words other than *not* are usually strong:

The sun never sets upon the British flag.

13. Omit needless words.

Vigorous writing is concise. A sentence should contain no unnecessary words, a paragraph no unnecessary sentences, for the same reason that a drawing should have no unnecessary lines and a machine no unnecessary parts. This requires not that the writer make all his sentences short, or that he avoid all detail and treat his subjects only in outline, but that every word tell.

Many expressions in common use violate this principle:

the question as to whether	whether (the question whether)
there is no doubt but that	no doubt (doubtless)
used for fuel purposes	used for fuel
he is a man who	he
in a hasty manner	hastily
this is a subject which	this subject
His story is a strange one.	His story is strange.

In especial the expression *the fact that* should be revised out of every sentence in which it occurs.

owing to the fact that	since (because)
in spite of the fact that	though (although)
call your attention to the fact that	remind you (notify you)
I was unaware of the fact that	I was unaware that (did not know)
the fact that he had not succeeded	his failure
the fact that I had arrived	my arrival

See also under case, character, nature, system in Chapter V.

Who is, which was, and the like are often superfluous.

> His brother, who is a member of the same firm

> His brother, a member of the same firm

> Trafalgar, which was Nelson's last battle

> Trafalgar, Nelson's last battle

As positive statement is more concise than negative, and the active voice more concise than the passive, many of the examples given under Rules 11 and 12 illustrate this rule as well.

A common violation of conciseness is the presentation of a single complex idea, step by step, in a series of sentences which might to advantage be combined into one.

> Macbeth was very ambitious. This led him to wish to become king of Scotland. The witches told him that this wish of his would come true. The king of Scotland at this time was Duncan. Encouraged by his wife, Macbeth murdered Duncan. He was thus enabled to succeed Duncan as king. (55 words.)

> Encouraged by his wife, Macbeth achieved his ambition and realized the prediction of the witches by murdering Duncan and becoming king of Scotland in his place. (26 words.)

14. Avoid a succession of loose sentences.

This rule refers especially to loose sentences of a particular type, those consisting of two co-ordinate clauses, the second introduced by a conjunction or relative. Although single sentences of this type may be unexceptionable (see under Rule 4), a series soon becomes monotonous and tedious.

An unskilful writer will sometimes construct a whole paragraph of sentences of this kind, using as connectives *and, but,* and less frequently, *who, which, when, where,* and *while,* these last in non-restrictive senses (see under Rule 3).

> The third concert of the subscription series was given last evening, and a large audience was in attendance. Mr. Edward Appleton was the soloist, and the Boston Symphony Orchestra furnished the instrumental music. The former showed

himself to be an artist of the first rank, while the latter proved itself fully deserving of its high reputation. The interest aroused by the series has been very gratifying to the Committee, and it is planned to give a similar series annually hereafter. The fourth concert will be given on Tuesday, May 10, when an equally attractive programme will be presented.

Apart from its triteness and emptiness, the paragraph above is bad because of the structure of its sentences, with their mechanical symmetry and sing-song. Contrast with them the sentences in the paragraphs quoted under Rule 10, or in any piece of good English prose, as the preface (Before the Curtain) to *Vanity Fair*.

If the writer finds that he has written a series of sentences of the type described, he should recast enough of them to remove the monotony, replacing them by simple sentences, by sentences of two clauses joined by a semicolon, by periodic sentences of two clauses, by sentences, loose or periodic, of three clauses—whichever best represent the real relations of the thought.

15. Express co-ordinate ideas in similar form.

This principle, that of parallel construction, requires that expressions of similar content and function should be outwardly similar. The likeness of form enables the reader to recognize more readily the likeness of content and function. Familiar instances from the Bible are the Ten Commandments, the Beatitudes, and the petitions of the Lord's Prayer.

The unskilful writer often violates this principle, from a mistaken belief that he should constantly vary the form of his expressions. It is true that in repeating a statement in order to emphasize it he may have need to vary its form. For illustration, see the paragraph from Stevenson quoted under Rule 10. But apart from this, he should follow the principle of parallel construction.

| Formerly, science was taught by the textbook method, while now the laboratory method is employed. | Formerly, science was taught by the textbook method; now it is taught by the laboratory method. |

The left-hand version gives the impression that the writer is undecided or timid; he seems unable or afraid to choose one form of expression and hold to it. The right-hand version shows that the writer has at least made his choice and abided by it.

By this principle, an article or a preposition applying to all the members of a series must either be used only before the first term or else be repeated before each term.

| The French, the Italians, Spanish, and Portuguese | The French, the Italians, the Spanish, and the Portuguese |
| In spring, summer, or in winter | In spring, summer, or winter (In spring, in summer, or in winter) |

Correlative expressions (*both, and; not, but; not only, but also; either, or; first, second, third;* and the like) should be followed by the same grammatical construction. Many violations of this rule can be corrected by rearranging the sentence.

It was both a long ceremony and very tedious.	The ceremony was both long and tedious.
A time not for words, but action	A time not for words, but for action
Either you must grant his request or incur his ill will.	You must either grant his request or incur his ill will.
My objections are, first, the injustice of the measure; second, that it is unconstitutional.	My objections are, first, that the measure is unjust; second, that it is unconstitutional.

See also the third example under Rule 12 and the last under Rule 13.

It may be asked, what if a writer needs to express a very large number of similar ideas, say twenty? Must he write twenty consecutive sentences of the same pattern? On closer examination he will probably find that the difficulty is imaginary, that his twenty ideas can be classified in groups, and that he need apply the principle only within each group. Otherwise he had best avoid the difficulty by putting his statements in the form of a table.

16. Keep related words together.

The position of the words in a sentence is the principal means of showing their relationship. The writer must therefore, so far as possible, bring together the words, and groups of words, that are related in thought, and keep apart those which are not so related.

The subject of a sentence and the principal verb should not, as a rule, be separated by a phrase or clause that can be transferred to the beginning.

Wordsworth, in the fifth book of *The Excursion,* gives a minute description of this church.	In the fifth book of *The Excursion,* Wordsworth gives a minute description of this church.
Cast iron, when treated in a Bessemer converter, is changed into steel.	By treatment in a Bessemer converter, cast iron is changed into steel.

The objection is that the interposed phrase or clause needlessly interrupts the natural order of the main clause. This objection, however, does not usually hold when the order is interrupted only by a relative clause or by an expression in apposition. Nor does it hold in periodic sentences in which the interruption is a deliberately used means of creating suspense (see examples under Rule 18).

The relative pronoun should come, as a rule, immediately after its antecedent.

There was a look in his eye that boded mischief.	In his eye was a look that boded mischief.
He wrote three articles about his adventures in Spain, which were published in *Harper's Magazine.*	He published in *Harper's Magazine* three articles about his adventures in Spain.
This is a portrait of Benjamin Harrison, grandson of William Henry Harrison, who became President in 1889.	This is a portrait of Benjamin Harrison, grandson of William Henry Harrison. He became President in 1889.

If the antecedent consists of a group of words, the relative comes at the end of the group, unless this would cause ambiguity.

>The Superintendent of the Chicago Division, who
>
>A proposal to amend the Sherman Act, which has been variously judged
>
>A proposal to amend the much-debated Sherman Act
>
>A proposal, which has been variously judged, to amend the Sherman Act
>
>The grandson of William Henry Harrison, who
>
>William Henry Harrison's grandson, Benjamin Harrison, who

A noun in apposition may come between antecedent and relative, because in such a combination no real ambiguity can arise.

The Duke of York, his brother, who was regarded with hostility by the Whigs

Modifiers should come, if possible next to the word they modify. If several expressions modify the same word, they should be so arranged that no wrong relation is suggested.

17. In summaries, keep to one tense.

>All the members were not present.
>
>Not all the members were present.
>
>He only found two mistakes.
>
>He found only two mistakes.
>
>Major R. E. Joyce will give a lecture on Tuesday evening in Bailey Hall, to which the public is invited, on "My Experiences in Mesopotamia" at eight P. M.
>
>On Tuesday evening at eight P. M., Major R. E. Joyce will give in Bailey Hall a lecture on "My Experiences in Mesopotamia." The public is invited.

In summarizing the action of a drama, the writer should always use the present tense. In summarizing a poem, story, or novel, he should preferably use the present, though he may use the past if he prefers. If the summary is in the present tense, antecedent action should be expressed by the perfect; if in the past, by the past perfect.

An unforeseen chance prevents Friar John from delivering Friar Lawrence's letter to Romeo. Juliet, meanwhile, owing to her father's arbitrary change of the day set for her wedding, has been compelled to drink the potion on Tuesday night, with the result that

Balthasar informs Romeo of her supposed death before Friar Lawrence learns of the nondelivery of the letter.

But whichever tense be used in the summary, a past tense in indirect discourse or in indirect question remains unchanged.

The Legate inquires who struck the blow.

Apart from the exceptions noted, whichever tense the writer chooses, he should use throughout. Shifting from one tense to the other gives the appearance of uncertainty and irresolution (compare Rule 15).

In presenting the statements or the thought of some one else, as in summarizing an essay or reporting a speech, the writer should avoid intercalating such expressions as "he said," "he stated," "the speaker added," "the speaker then went on to say," "the author also thinks," or the like. He should indicate clearly at the outset, once for all, that what follows is summary, and then waste no words in repeating the notification.

In notebooks, in newspapers, in handbooks of literature, summaries of one kind or another may be indispensable, and for children in primary schools it is a useful exercise to retell a story in their own words. But in the criticism or interpretation of literature the writer should be careful to avoid dropping into summary. He may find it necessary to devote one or two sentences to indicating the subject, or the opening situation, of the work he is discussing; he may cite numerous details to illustrate its qualities. But he should aim to write an orderly discussion supported by evidence, not a summary with occasional comment. Similarly, if the scope of his discussion includes a number of works, he will as a rule do better not to take them up singly in chronological order, but to aim from the beginning at establishing general conclusions.

18. Place the emphatic words of a sentence at the end.

The proper place for the word, or group of words, which the writer desires to make most prominent is usually the end of the sentence.

Humanity has hardly advanced in fortitude since that time, though it has advanced in many other ways.	Humanity, since that time, has advanced in many other ways, but it has hardly advanced in fortitude.
This steel is principally used for making razors, because of its hardness.	Because of its hardness, this steel is principally used in making razors.

The word or group of words entitled to this position of prominence is usually the logical predicate, that is, the *new* element in the sentence, as it is in the second example.

The effectiveness of the periodic sentence arises from the prominence which it gives to the main statement.

Four centuries ago, Christopher Columbus, one of the Italian mariners whom the decline of their own republics had put at the service of the world and of adventure, seeking for Spain a westward passage to the Indies as a set-off against the achievements of Portuguese discoverers, lighted on America.
With these hopes and in this belief I would urge you, laying aside all hindrance, thrusting away all private aims, to devote yourselves unswervingly and unflinchingly to the vigorous and successful prosecution of this war.

The other prominent position in the sentence is the beginning. Any element in the sentence, other than the subject, becomes emphatic when placed first.

Deceit or treachery he could never forgive.
So vast and rude, fretted by the action of nearly three thousand years, the fragments of this architecture may often seem, at first sight, like works of nature.

A subject coming first in its sentence may be emphatic, but hardly by its position alone. In the sentence,

Great kings worshipped at his shrine,
the emphasis upon *kings* arises largely from its meaning and from the context. To receive special emphasis, the subject of a sentence must take the position of the predicate.

Through the middle of the valley flowed a winding stream.

Write the Perfect Research Paper

The principle that the proper place for what is to be made most prominent is the end applies equally to the words of a sentence, to the sentences of a paragraph, and to the paragraphs of a composition.

IV. A Few Matters of Form

Headings. Leave a blank line, or its equivalent in space, after the title or heading of a manuscript. On succeeding pages, if using ruled paper, begin on the first line.

Numerals. Do not spell out dates or other serial numbers. Write them in figures or in Roman notation, as may be appropriate.

August 9, 1918 Chapter XII

Rule 3   352d Infantry

Parentheses. A sentence containing an expression in parenthesis is punctuated, outside of the marks of parenthesis, exactly as if the expression in parenthesis were absent. The expression within is punctuated as if it stood by itself, except that the final stop is omitted unless it is a question mark or an exclamation point.

I went to his house yesterday (my third attempt to see him), but he had left town.
He declares (and why should we doubt his good faith?) that he is now certain of success.

(When a wholly detached expression or sentence is parenthesized, the final stop comes before the last mark of parenthesis.)

Quotations. Formal quotations, cited as documentary evidence, are introduced by a colon and enclosed in quotation marks.

The provision of the Constitution is: "No tax or duty shall be laid on articles exported from any state."
Quotations grammatically in apposition or the direct objects of verbs are preceded by a comma and enclosed in quotation marks.

I recall the maxim of La Rochefoucauld, "Gratitude is a lively sense of benefits to come."
Aristotle says, "Art is an imitation of nature."

Quotations of an entire line, or more, of verse, are begun on a fresh line and centred, but not enclosed in quotation marks.

Wordsworth's enthusiasm for the Revolution was at first unbounded:
Bliss was it in that dawn to be alive,
But to be young was very heaven!

Quotations introduced by *that* are regarded as in indirect discourse and not enclosed in quotation marks.

Keats declares that beauty is truth, truth beauty.
Proverbial expressions and familiar phrases of literary origin require no quotation marks.

These are the times that try men's souls.
He lives far from the madding crowd.

The same is true of colloquialisms and slang.

References. In scholarly work requiring exact references, abbreviate titles that occur frequently, giving the full forms in an alphabetical list at the end. As a general practice, give the references in parenthesis or in footnotes, not in the body of the sentence. Omit the words *act, scene, line, book, volume, page,* except when referring by only one of them. Punctuate as indicated below.

| In the second scene of the third act | In III.ii (still better, simply insert III.ii in parenthesis at the proper place in the sentence) |

After the killing of Polonius, Hamlet is placed under guard (IV. ii. 14).

2 *Samuel* i:17-27   *Othello* II.iii 264-267, III.iii. 155-161

Titles. For the titles of literary works, scholarly usage prefers italics with capitalized initials. The usage of editors and publishers varies, some using italics with capitalized initials, others using Roman with capitalized initials and with or without quotation marks. Use italics (indicated in manuscript by underscoring), except in writing for a periodical that follows a different practice. Omit initial *A* or *The* from titles when you place the possessive before them.

The *Iliad;* the *Odyssey; As You Like It; To a Skylark; The Newcomes; A Tale of Two Cities;* Dicken's *Tale of Two Cities.*

V. Words and Expressions Commonly Misused

(Many of the words and expressions here listed are not so much bad English as bad style, the commonplaces of careless writing. As illustrated under *Feature,* the proper correction is likely to be not the replacement of one word or set of words by another, but the replacement of vague generality by definite statement.)

All right. Idiomatic in familiar speech as a detached phrase in the sense, "Agreed," or "Go ahead." In other uses better avoided. Always written as two words.

As good or better than. Expressions of this type should be corrected by rearranging the sentence.

My opinion is as good or better than his.   My opinion is as good as his, or better (if not better).

As to whether. *Whether* is sufficient; see under Rule 13.

Bid. Takes the infinitive without *to.* The past tense is *bade.*

Case. The *Concise Oxford Dictionary* begins its definition of this word: "instance of a thing's occurring; usual state of affairs." In these two senses, the word is usually unnecessary.

In many cases, the rooms were poorly ventilated.   Many of the rooms were poorly ventilated.

It has rarely been the case that any mistake has been made.   Few mistakes have been made.

See Wood, *Suggestions to Authors,* pp. 68-71, and Quiller-Couch, *The Art of Writing,* pp. 103-106.

Certainly. Used indiscriminately by some speakers, much as others use <u>very</u>, to intensify any and every statement. A mannerism of this kind, bad in speech, is even worse in writing.

Character. Often simply redundant, used from a mere habit of wordiness.

Acts of a hostile character Hostile acts

Claim, vb. With object-noun, means *lay claim to.* May be used with a dependent clause if this sense is clearly involved: "He claimed that he was the sole surviving heir." (But even here, "claimed to be" would be better.) Not to be used as a substitute for *declare, maintain,* or *charge.*

Compare. To *compare to* is to point out or imply resemblances, between objects regarded as essentially of different order; to *compare with* is mainly to point out differences, between objects regarded as essentially of the same order. Thus life has been compared to a pilgrimage, to a drama, to a battle; Congress may be compared with the British Parliament. Paris has been compared to ancient Athens; it may be compared with modern London.

Clever. This word has been greatly overused; it is best restricted to ingenuity displayed in small matters.

Consider. Not followed by *as* when it means, "believe to be." "I consider him thoroughly competent." Compare, "The lecturer considered Cromwell first as soldier and second as administrator," where "considered" means "examined" or "discussed."

Dependable. A needless substitute for *reliable, trustworthy.*

Due to. Incorrectly used for *through, because of,* or *owing to,* in adverbial phrases: "He lost the first game, due to carelessness." In correct use related as predicate or as modifier to a particular noun: "This invention is due to Edison;" "losses due to preventable fires."

Effect. As noun, means *result;* as verb, means *to bring about, accomplish* (not to be confused with *affect,* which means "to influence").

As noun, often loosely used in perfunctory writing about fashions, music, painting, and other arts: "an Oriental effect;" "effects in pale green;" "very delicate effects;" "broad effects;" "subtle effects;" "a charming effect was produced by." The writer who has a definite meaning to express will not take refuge in such vagueness.

Etc. Not to be used of persons. Equivalent to *and the rest, and so forth,* and hence not to be used if one of these would be insufficient, that is, if the reader would be left in doubt as to any important particulars. Least open to objection when it represents the last terms of a list already given in full, or immaterial words at the end of a quotation.

At the end of a list introduced by *such as, for example,* or any similar expression, *etc.* is incorrect.

Fact. Use this word only of matters of a kind capable of direct verification, not of matters of judgment. That a particular event happened on a given date, that lead melts at a certain temperature, are facts. But such conclusions as that Napoleon was the greatest of modern generals, or that the climate of California is delightful, however incontestable they may be, are not properly facts.

On the formula *the fact that,* see under Rule 13.

Factor. A hackneyed word; the expressions of which it forms part can usually be replaced by something more direct and idiomatic.

| His superior training was the great factor in his winning the match. | He won the match by being better trained. |
| Heavy artillery is becoming an increasingly important factor in deciding battles. | Heavy artillery is playing a larger and larger part in deciding battles. |

Feature. Another hackneyed word; like *factor* it usually adds nothing to the sentence in which it occurs.

A feature of the entertainment especially worthy of mention was the singing of Miss A.

(Better use the same number of words to tell what Miss A. sang, or if the programme has already been given, to tell something of how she sang.)

As a verb, in the advertising sense of *offer as a special attraction,* to be avoided.

Fix. Colloquial in America for *arrange, prepare, mend.* In writing restrict it to its literary senses, *fasten, make firm or immovable,* etc.

He is a man who. A common type of redundant expression; see Rule 13.

He is a man who is very ambitious.

He is very ambitious.

Spain is a country which I have always wanted to visit.

I have always wanted to visit Spain.

However. In the meaning *nevertheless,* not to come first in its sentence or clause.

The roads were almost impassable. However, we at last succeeded in reaching camp.

The roads were almost impassable. At last, however, we succeeded in reaching camp.

When *however* comes first, it means *in whatever way* or *to whatever extent.*

However you advise him, he will probably do as he thinks best.
However discouraging the prospect, he never lost heart.

Kind of. Not to be used as a substitute for *rather* (before adjectives and verbs), or except in familiar style, for *something like* (before nouns). Restrict it to its literal sense: "Amber is a kind of fossil resin;" "I dislike that kind of notoriety." The same holds true of *sort of.*

Less. Should not be misused for *fewer.*

He had less men than in the previous campaign.

He had fewer men than in the previous campaign.

Less refers to quantity, *fewer* to number. "His troubles are less than mine" means "His troubles are not so great as mine." "His troubles are fewer than mine" means "His troubles are not so numerous as mine." It is, however, correct to say, "The signers of the petition were less than a hundred, "where the round number, a hundred, is something like a collective noun, and *less* is thought of as meaning a less quantity or amount.

Line, along these lines. *Line* in the sense of *course of procedure, conduct, thought,* is allowable, but has been so much overworked, particularly in the phrase *along these lines,* that a writer who aims at freshness or originality had better discard it entirely.

Mr. B. also spoke along the same lines.	Mr. B. also spoke, to the same effect.
He is studying along the line of French literature.	He is studying French literature.

Literal, literally. Often incorrectly used in support of exaggeration or violent metaphor.

A literal flood of abuse	A flood of abuse
Literally dead with fatigue	Almost dead with fatigue (dead tired)

Lose out. Meant to be more emphatic than *lose,* but actually less so, because of its commonness. The same holds true of *try out, win out, sign up, register up.* With a number of verbs, *out* and *up* form idiomatic combinations: *find out, run out, turn out, cheer up, dry up, make up,* and others, each distinguishable in meaning from the simple verb. *Lose out* is not.

Most. Not to be used for *almost.*

Most everybody	Almost everybody
Most all the time	Almost all the time

Nature. Often simply redundant, used like *character*.

Acts of a hostile nature   Hostile acts

Often vaguely used in such expressions as "a lover of nature;" "poems about nature." Unless more specific statements follow, the reader cannot tell whether the poems have to do with natural scenery, rural life, the sunset, the untracked wilderness, or the habits of squirrels.

Near by. Adverbial phrase, not yet fully accepted as good English, though the analogy of *close by* and *hard by* seems to justify it. *Near, or near at hand,* is as good, if not better.

Not to be used as an adjective; use *neighboring.*

Oftentimes, ofttimes. Archaic forms, no longer in good use. The modern word is *often.*

One hundred and one. Retain the *and* in this and similar expressions, in accordance with the unvarying usage of English prose from Old English times.

One of the most. Avoid beginning essays or paragraphs with this formula, as, "One of the most interesting developments of modern science is, etc.;" "Switzerland is one of the most interesting countries of Europe." There is nothing wrong in this; it is simply threadbare and forcible-feeble.

People. *The people* is a political term, not to be confused with *the public.* From the people comes political support or opposition; from the public comes artistic appreciation or commercial patronage.

The word *people* is not to be used with words of number, in place of *persons.* If of "six people" five went away, how many "people" would be left?

Phase. Means a stage of transition or development: "the phases of the moon;" "the last phase." Not to be used for *aspect* or *topic.*

| Another phase of the subject | Another point (another question) |

Possess. Not to be used as a mere substitute for *have* or *own.*

| He possessed great courage. | He had great courage (was very brave). |
| He was the fortunate possessor of | He owned |

Respective, respectively. These words may usually be omitted with advantage.

Write the Perfect Research Paper

Works of fiction are listed under the names of their respective authors.	Works of fiction are listed under the names of their authors.
The one mile and two mile runs were won by Jones and Cummings respectively.	The one mile and two mile runs were won by Jones and by Cummings.

In some kinds of formal writing, as in geometrical proofs, it may be necessary to use *respectively,* but it should not appear in writing on ordinary subjects.

So. Avoid, in writing, the use of *so* as an intensifier: "so good;" "so warm;" "so delightful."

On the use of *so* to introduce clauses, see <u>Rule 4</u>.

Sort of. See under <u>Kind of</u>.

State. Not to be used as a mere substitute for *say, remark.* Restrict it to the sense of *express fully or clearly,* as, "He refused to state his objections."

Learner body. A needless and awkward expression, meaning no more than the simple word *learners.*

A member of the learner body	A learner
Popular with the learner body	Liked by the learners
The learner body passed resolutions.	The learners passed resolutions.

System. Frequently used without need.

Dayton has adopted the commission system of government.	Dayton has adopted government by commission.
The dormitory system	Dormitories

Thanking you in advance. This sounds as if the writer meant, "It will not be worth my while to write to you again." Simply write, "Thanking you," and if the favor which you have requested is granted, write a letter of acknowledgment.

They. A common inaccuracy is the use of the plural pronoun when the antecedent is a distributive expression such as *each, each one, everybody, every one, many a man,* which, though implying more than one person, requires the pronoun to be in the singular. Similar to this, but with even less justification, is the use of the plural pronoun with the antecedent *anybody, any one, somebody, some one,* the intention being either to avoid the awkward "he or she," or to avoid committing oneself to either. Some bashful speakers even say, "A friend of mine told me that they, etc."

Use *he* with all the above words, unless the antecedent is or must be feminine.

Very. Use this word sparingly. Where emphasis is necessary, use words strong in themselves.

Viewpoint. Write *point of view,* but do not misuse this, as many do, for *view* or *opinion.*

While. Avoid the indiscriminate use of this word for *and, but,* and *although.* Many writers use it frequently as a substitute for *and* or *but,* either from a mere desire to vary the connective, or from uncertainty which of the two connectives is the more appropriate. In this use it is best replaced by a semicolon.

| The office and salesrooms are on the ground floor, while the rest of the building is devoted to manufacturing. | The office and salesrooms are on the ground floor; the rest of the building is devoted to manufacturing. |

Its use as a virtual equivalent of *although* is allowable in sentences where this leads to no ambiguity or absurdity.

While I admire his energy, I wish it were employed in a better cause.
This is entirely correct, as shown by the paraphrase,

I admire his energy; at the same time I wish it were employed in a better cause.
Compare:

While the temperature reaches 90 or 95 degrees in the daytime, the nights are often chilly.	Although the temperature reaches 90 or 95 degrees in the daytime, the nights are often chilly.

The paraphrase,

The temperature reaches 90 or 95 degrees in the daytime; at the same time the nights are often chilly,

shows why the use of *while* is incorrect.

In general, the writer will do well to use *while* only with strict literalness, in the sense of *during the time that*.

Whom. Often incorrectly used for *who* before *he said* or similar expressions, when it is really the subject of a following verb.

His brother, whom he said would send him the money	His brother, who he said would send him the money
The man whom he thought was his friend	The man who (that) he thought was his friend (whom he thought his friend)

Worth while. Overworked as a term of vague approval and (with *not*) of disapproval. Strictly applicable only to actions: "Is it worth while to telegraph?"

His books are not worth while.	His books are not worth reading (not worth one's while to read; do not repay reading).

The use of *worth while* before a noun ("a worth while story") is indefensible.

Would. A conditional statement in the first person requires *should*, not *would*.

I should not have succeeded without his help.

The equivalent of *shall* in indirect quotation after a verb in the past tense is *should*, not *would*.

He predicted that before long we should have a great surprise.

To express habitual or repeated action, the past tense, without *would,* is usually sufficient, and from its brevity, more emphatic.

Once a year he would visit the old mansion.

Once a year he visited the old mansion.

VI. Words Often Misspelled

accidentally	formerly	privilege
advice	humorous	pursue
affect	hypocrisy	repetition
beginning	immediately	rhyme
believe	incidentally	rhythm
benefit	latter	ridiculous
challenge	led	sacrilegious
criticize	lose	seize
deceive	marriage	separate
definite	mischief	shepherd
describe	murmur	siege
despise	necessary	similar
develop	occurred	simile
disappoint	parallel	too
duel	Philip	tragedy
ecstasy	playwright	tries
effect	preceding	undoubtedly
existence	prejudice	until

fiery   principal

Write *to-day, to-night, to-morrow* (but not *together*) with hyphen.

Write *any one, every one, some one, some time* (except the sense of *formerly*) as two words.

THE END

About the Author:

Cheryl Carter is an adjunct English professor with a passion to help all students do well in English. She believes all students can do well, if they are adequately prepared for college writing. Carter is a freelance writer and author. She has successfully helped many international students improve their writing and gain entry into some of the most competitive and elite colleges in the United States. Besides teaching, she tutors students in English and language arts. She has a Certificate of College Admission Advisement from Columbia University. Contact her at Cheryl@Writeforcollege.org

Made in the USA
Columbia, SC
06 October 2023